John Dennis

Twayne's English Authors Series

Bertram H. Davis, Editor

Florida State University

TEAS 382

JOHN DENNIS (1658–1734)
Engraving by Jan Van der Gucht
Reproduced by permission of
The Huntington Library, San Marino, CA.
Print Collection Box 75, 59:2

John Dennis

By Avon Jack Murphy

Northeast Louisiana University

Twayne Publishers • *Boston*

John Dennis

Avon Jack Murphy

Copyright © 1984 by G. K. Hall & Company
All Rights Reserved
Published by Twayne Publishers
A Division of G. K. Hall & Company
70 Lincoln Street
Boston, Massachusetts 02111

Book Production by Marne B. Sultz
Book Design by Barbara Anderson

Printed on permanent/durable acid-free
paper and bound in the United States of
America.

**Library of Congress Cataloging in
Publication Data**

Murphy, Avon Jack.
    John Dennis.

    (Twayne's English authors series; TEAS 382)
    Bibliography: p.   143
    Includes index.
    1. Dennis, John, 1657–1734—Criticism and interpretation.
    2. Criticism—Great Britain—History—17th century.
    I. Title.   II. Series.
PR3409.D3Z78   1984   809   84–9132
ISBN 0–8057–6868–8

Contents

About the Author
Preface
Acknowledgment
Chronology

Chapter One
Life   1

Chapter Two
General Literary Criticism   7

Chapter Three
Evaluation of Fellow Authors   16

Chapter Four
Plays   66

Chapter Five
Poetry   90

Chapter Six
Noncritical Prose   109

Chapter Seven
Toward an Appreciation of Dennis   129

Notes and References   133
Selected Bibliography   143
Index   151

About the Author

Avon Jack Murphy is an associate professor of English at Northeast Louisiana University. A native of Oregon, he earned the Ph.D. at the University of Wisconsin–Madison. His research has focused on seventeenth-century poetry, children's literature, contemporary fiction, and technical writing. He and his wife, Virginia, have two sons.

Preface

For most readers familiar with his name, John Dennis means two things. First, he embodies the stereotypical Neoclassical literary critic. He wrote, after all, treatises like *The Advancement and Reformation of Modern Poetry* and *The Grounds of Criticism in Poetry,* full of such abstract topics as the dramatic unities and the genres. Second, he often wrote stodgily, vainly, or even viciously, fully deserving the ridicule heaped upon him in Pope's *The Dunciad.*

Closer study reveals a career far richer and more positive than this facile and largely inaccurate capsule verdict suggests. True, Dennis succeeded most conspicuously as a critic—contemporary writers awarded him the title "the Critic"—but he also published a large body of poems, letters, plays, and what I call noncritical prose, various pamphlets devoted more to social, political, and religious than to literary matters. And while the writer's personality may not have proven wholly attractive, he possessed definite strengths of character; even most of the defects seem less serious when we discover their contexts.

In assessing Dennis's achievement, I have avoided the temptation to treat him as a magnificent compendium of information about the English literary scene of the 1690s through the 1720s. He is that indeed: he tells us much about such workaday details as the composition of playhouse audiences and the prices of theater seats; and he provides details about William Wycherley, Elkanah Settle, John Crowne, and others that their biographers must use. In fact, such fine modern critics as John Loftis and Emmett L. Avery often cite his testimony to verify statements of fact. However, I wish instead to concentrate on the variety and unity that make the career of John Dennis so much fuller than most earlier writers have recognized.

I might explain my procedure in some of the following chapters. I take pains in chapter 2 to outline critical principles enunciated in the general critical treatises because those principles underlie all of Dennis's work, not just his criticism. In chapter 3 I do not devote a great deal of space to his letters on Shakespeare and Milton since I return to his reflections upon those authors in other chapters, and many other critics have described the letters; I devote several pages to Pope, since the Pope-Dennis warfare so greatly affected Dennis's career and reputation. And in chapter 6 I describe fully the naval pamphlets because they best reflect his dictum that writers must always serve the public interest.

I owe numerous people thanks for their help. The Andrew W. Mellon Foundation granted a fellowship to the William Andrews Clark Library, where William Conway and his staff made research pleasant; Noelle Jackson of the Henry E. Huntington Library proved as helpful as ever. Mary Bower and other friends at Ferris State College helped more than they may realize; also, a sabbatical leave made possible the impossible. The Newberry Library and the libraries at Central Michigan University and the University of Michigan contributed much appreciated assistance. Finally, Gini and the boys were always there.

NOTE: throughout my discussion I abbreviate the titles of three books. *CW* = *The Critical Works of John Dennis; SW* = *The Select Works of Mr. John Dennis; OL* = *Original Letters.*

Avon Jack Murphy

Northeast Louisiana University

Acknowledgment

I thank the Johns Hopkins University Press for permission to use quotations from Edward Niles Hooker's two-volume edition of *The Critical Works of John Dennis* (1939–43).

Chronology

1658   John Dennis born 16 September in London to Francis and Sarah Dennis.

1679   Bachelor of Arts, Caius College, Cambridge.

1683   Master of Arts, Trinity College, Cambridge.

1688   Tour of France and Italy.

1692   Poems in the *Gentleman's Journal; Poems in Burlesque; Poems and Letters upon Several Occasions; The Passion of Byblis;* knew Dryden and Wycherley.

1693   *The Impartial Critick; Miscellanies in Verse and Prose.*

1695   *The Court of Death.*

1696   *Remarks on a Book Entituled, Prince Arthur; Letters upon Several Occasions.*

1697   *A Plot, and No Plot; The Nuptials of Britain's Genius and Fame; Miscellany Poems.*

1698   *The Usefulness of the Stage;* translation of one book of *The Annals and History of Cornelius Tacitus;* impoverished; almost indicted by the Middlesex grand jury.

1699   *Rinaldo and Armida.*

1700   *Iphigenia; The Seamens Case; The Reverse;* Parliamentary work for sailors.

1701   *The Advancement and Reformation of Modern Poetry.*

1702   *The Comical Gallant* (published with *A Large Account of the Taste in Poetry*); *The Danger of Priestcraft to Religion and Government; An Essay on the Navy; The Monument;* attacked by Henry Sacheverell.

1703   *A Proposal for Putting a Speedy End to the War.*

1704   *The Grounds of Criticism in Poetry; The Person of Quality's Answer to Mr. Collier's Letter; Liberty Asserted; Britannia Triumphans.*

1705   *Gibraltar;* given post as royal waiter in the London Custom-House.

1706   *An Essay on the Opera's; The Battle of Ramillia.*

1707   Contributions to *The Muses Mercury.*

1709   *Appius and Virginia.*

1711–1715   Legal difficulties because of indebtedness.

1711   *Reflections . . . upon . . . An Essay upon Criticism; An Essay upon Publick Spirit;* attacked in Alexander Pope's *An Essay on Criticism* and *The Critical Specimen;* beginning of feud with Richard Steele.

1712   *An Essay on the Genius and Writings of Shakespear.*

1713   *Remarks upon Cato;* attacked in Pope's *Narrative of Dr. Robert Norris.*

1714   *A Poem upon the Death of . . . Queen Anne, and the . . . Accession of . . . King George.*

1715   *Priestcraft Distinguish'd from Christianity.*

1716   *A True Character of Mr. Pope, and His Writings.*

1717   *Remarks upon Mr. Pope's Translation of Homer.*

1718   *The Select Works.*

1719   Discussed in Giles Jacob's *Poetical Register.*

1720   *The Invader of His Country; The Characters and Conduct of Sir John Edgar;* sells his Custom-House post.

1721   *Original Letters.*

1722   *A Defence of Sir Fopling Flutter;* "Of Prosody"; *Julius Caesar Acquitted, and His Murderers Condemn'd.*

1723   *Remarks on . . . The Conscious Lovers.*

1724–1725   Letters in the *Plain Dealer.*

1724   *Vice and Luxury Publick Mischiefs;* defended in the *Plain Dealer.*

ca. 1725   *The Causes of the Decay and Defects of Dramatick Poetry* (1943).

1726   *The Stage Defended.*

1727   *Miscellaneous Tracts.*

1728   *Remarks on Mr. Pope's Rape of the Lock; The Faith*

and Duties of Christians; attacked in Pope's *The Dunciad.*

1729 *Remarks upon . . . the Dunciad.*

1730 *A Treatise Concerning the State of Departed Souls;* unsuccessful candidate for Poet Laureate.

1733 Benefit performance for Dennis of Vanbrugh's *The Provok'd Husband,* with a prologue by Pope.

1734 Dies London, 6 January; *The Life of Mr. John Dennis.*

Chapter One

Life

John Dennis was born on 16 September 1658 in the parish of St. Andrew's Holborn, London.[1] He was the only child of Francis Dennis, a successful saddler, and Sarah Dennis. After his father's death in 1663, his widowed mother married Thomas Sanderson, also a saddler. From this union resulted Dennis's half sister, Elizabeth. One scholar has said that a shadowy "Mr. Smith" was his brother.[2] Perhaps this was a half brother or Elizabeth's husband; we do not know her married name.

The renowned Dr. William Horne supervised Dennis's education at Harrow-on-the-Hill. On 13 January 1676 he entered Caius College, Cambridge, where he remained as a common scholar until 1680 and received the B.A. in 1679. We find at this early date the first of the numerous stories smacking of both fact and fiction that complicate his biography. The Cambridge *Gesta Book* states that on 4 March 1680 "Sir Dennis" (probably John Dennis) was fined, deprived of his scholarship, and expelled from Caius for stabbing a fellow student. This story, first recorded by David Erskine Baker and thought sufficiently entertaining by John Nichols to reproduce in *Literary Anecdotes of the Eighteenth Century* (1812), appears to be a true one. In any case, Dennis transferred to Trinity Hall (with its high reputation for scholarship) in 1681, receiving the M.A. in 1683. Here he probably remained as a tutor until 1686; he seems also to have been incorporated at Oxford in 1683.[3]

Fred S. Tupper has uncovered specific details about the young scholar's finances. His wealthy uncle Simon Eve in 1670 bequeathed him five hundred pounds, and in 1673 Thomas Sanderson bequeathed him fifty pounds. A 1686 chancery suit brought by Dennis against his mother indicates some extravagance on his part and withholding of money on hers. We do not know the verdict, but he doubtless received a settlement.

By 1688 his finances were strong enough to let Dennis tour

the Continent. Letters written from Paris, Lyons, Turin, and Rome reveal the young man forming opinions that he would never discard. We have, for instance, his famous letter on finding sublimity in the Alps. And he already loathes the French, because "The *French* then are affected and impudent, which are but the necessary effects of that National Vice, their Vanity" (*Miscellanies,* 129).

Upon his return from his travels, Dennis strove to join the literary establishment. Now thirty years old, he had to his credit only one inconsequential poem, but he soon changed this record. *Letters upon Several Occasions* (1696) show him working feverishly during 1694 and 1695 to establish strong personal connections with such men as Dryden, Wycherley, Congreve, and Walter Moyle. From approximately 1690 into the late 1690s, he set himself up as a witty man of letters familiar with Thomas D'Urfey, Thomas Cheek, and other fellow wits at Will's and other coffeehouses. The early poetry found in *Poems in Burlesque* (1692) and *Miscellanies in Verse and Prose* (1693) demonstrates the railing tone popular with rising young gallants, while letters not only feature the same tone but refer directly to coffeehouse gossip and boast of membership in "the *Witty Club*" (as in *SW*, 2:531, 537). As if to signify his arrival, the *Gentleman's Journal* in 1692 advertises his growing reputation, and he is attacked in Richard Blackmore's *A Satyr against Wit* (1699) and Defoe's *The Pacificator* (1700), in which he commands the forces of wit.

By 1700, however, he no longer claimed status as a wit, for two major reasons. First, he could not afford the life of a gallant. Defending herself in the 1686 suit, his mother claims, "Haveing by his extravagancie spent and consumed his fortune and haveing nothing to live on and being reduced to necessity this Def^t was forced . . . to help him to money clothes and other necessaries and pay for his tabling and board. . . ."[4] Such extravagance and consequent poverty haunted him through most of his life. A John Dennis, who may be our man, was imprisoned for debt in the Fleet in 1696. We know that two years later, when the Middlesex grand jury was ready to prosecute him for libelous statements in *The Usefulness of the Stage,* William Aglionby wanted to help get the "poor poet" money to defend himself.

Second, because of both the moral-reform trends of the time and his own character, Dennis early conceived of a more serious literary mission than entertaining fellow wits. One of the focal points in *The Usefulness* is that literature can strengthen government and religion. Soon we find him insisting in prefaces and title pages that he is writing for the good of his country, *The Seamens Case* (1700?), for instance, being signed "Philo Patriae." He goes on in plays to make his virtuous characters mouth like sentiments and to work out poetic justice. Dennis tries also to write a higher poetry, which Dryden feels that Dennis can master (*SW*, 2:504); such poetry will marvelously improve its readers. He also seems destined from his early professional years to become a serious literary critic. *The Impartial Critick* (1693), although written in a somewhat bantering dialogue format, addresses major critical concerns, and several early letters discuss similar topics, as when in 1695 he speculates with Moyle about dramatic rules. He composes such works as the *Remarks* on Blackmore (1696), *The Usefulness,* and *The Advancement and Reformation of Modern Poetry* (1701), so that by 1704 the author of *The Tryal of Skill* expresses the accepted view by labeling Dennis "the Critick."

The years 1700–1710 mark the high point of Dennis's life and career. The public accepted him as an outstanding critic. He served the public and the Whig cause well (although he never became a party hack writer) with Parliamentary lobbying and pamphlets on behalf of sailors, *The Danger of Priestcraft* (1702), *A Proposal for Putting a Speedy End to the War* (1703), *An Essay on the Opera's* (1706), and other works. By 1710 he had produced seven plays, one of them, *Liberty Asserted,* a popular success. And very importantly, he temporarily overcame his financial problems, no extant documents indicating prison terms for indebtedness. In 1705 the Duke of Marlborough, grateful for the praise lavished in *Britannia Triumphans* (1704), gave Dennis money and exerted influence to get him a post as a royal waiter, or undersearcher, for the Port of London. This, Dennis's only political position, required little work but yielded 120 pounds annually.

Around 1710, however, Dennis's fortunes began a marked decline. Massive evidence documents his slide into poverty. From at least 1710 he worked as a notary public, an office through which he somehow entangled himself in lawsuits accusing him of defrauding sailors of wages he had collected for them. He went through formal bankruptcy proceedings in 1711. As matters became worse, he spent time serving sentences for debt or evading the authorities. He applied for discharge from the Fleet in 1712. Two years later Swift satirically portrays Dennis inviting Steele to escape "Dunns and Debts," while a poem erroneously ascribed to Swift has Dennis similarly inviting Steele "to come and live with him in the Mint," the Southwark debtors' sanctuary.[5] Theophilus Cibber tells an anecdote illustrating the legendary furtiveness growing out of factual necessity. It seems that Dennis one Saturday night sat long in a pub, eyeing a suspicious-looking man whom he feared to be a bailiff ready to capture him; at midnight Dennis erupted, "Now sir, Bailiff, or no Bailiff, I don't care a farthing for you, you have no power now."[6] Perhaps Dennis's many changes of address stem from his attempts to evade such men.

Dennis had to find a way to eliminate his debts. His solution was to sell his customs post. Secretary of State James Stanhope helped "poor Dennis the Poet" toward this end in 1715, and by 1720 the post was indeed sold. Unfortunately, this transaction by no means solved his whole problem, for we hear much of his poverty until his death. Thanking a friend in 1720 for help against his brother-in-law, Dennis acknowledges, "I have all my life time had but a little" money (*OL,* 1:46). In his last years numerous writers allude to his dire poverty, sometimes with pity, often with savageness, as in one wit's jibe about "Old *Dennis*" begging for his supper or in the final lines of an epigram:

> Of one so poor you cannot take the law;
> On one so old your sword you scorn to draw.
> Uncag'd then let the harmless Monster rage,
> Secure in dullness, madness, want, and age.[7]

As poverty harassed the aging Dennis, so did frequent ill health. His letters mention gout, fever, stones, increasing weight, and unspecified bouts of "great and dangerous Indisposition." Most alarming perhaps were visual problems. He apologized in 1713 for returning a friend's Cicero because he could not read the small print (*OL,* 1:197), and before his death he was blind.

Even more damaging in the later years was the sinking of his reputation through quarrels with other writers. Before 1710 he suffered the kinds of attack that any well-known eighteenth-century writer would expect. Thus, the prologue to Abel Boyer's *Achilles* (1700) satirizes his "*Tremendous*" lines because the style of Dennis's *Iphigenia* seems to call for such criticism, Henry Sacheverell's *The New Association* (1702) attacks Dennis in response to the attack in *The Danger of Priestcraft,* and Dennis is grouped with many other writers (including Dryden and Congreve) for attack in Matthew Coppinger's (?) *A Session of the Poets* (1705).

After 1710, however, Dennis's character combined with other factors to initiate vicious feuding, especially with Pope and Steele, as will be discussed in chapter 2. Pope more than anyone else launched savage attacks that in their totality destroyed for generations the good name Dennis had carefully built. Inventing a personal history and a set of personal qualities, Pope gave the public a fully characterized Dennis bearing little relation to fact but made credible by the finely executed lines and solid mass of consistent "facts." Because Dennis could not effectively counter Pope's brilliant portraiture, most readers came to see Dennis as a stereotypical dunce, unfeeling, irascible, unable to judge literature except by unbreakable rules, insensitive to connotations, vengeful, unable to judge himself, and limited in interests.

Since he did not command Pope's verbal skills, Dennis replied to attacks by Pope and others with too much irascibility and insensitivity to connotations—as if he had become what Pope said he was. This we see in works like *The Characters and Conduct of Sir John Edgar, Remarks upon Cato,* and the pamphlets against Pope, all at least in part conceived as rebuttals to unwarranted attacks. Contemporary readers, then, found Dennis being described negatively by opposing authors and characterizing himself negatively through his responses. Still other writers fell in with what quickly became tradition: the aging writer deserved ridicule. Gay, Fielding, John Arbuthnot, Richard Victor—many seem to assail Dennis because they feel expected to do so.

Dennis attempted to reverse the slide with a two-volume edition of his works, which he began to prepare in 1716. He told Steele in 1719 his two motives. First "was the Apprehension I had of the Danger, which the Liberties of my Country were in, and consequently the Liberties of the Christian World. . . . I wrote them . . . as a Lover of my Country, and one zealous to promote the Happiness of *Great Britain.*" Second, he wished to preserve his writings, especially since "they were in a great many different Hands, and some of them in the Hands of such who were mortal Enemies to the Cause in which they were written" (*CW,* 2:172–73). Unfortunately, by the time Dennis published *The Select Works* (1718), his decline in reputation greatly restricted sales. The publisher tried in 1721 "unloading an overstock of the unsold work of the sometime popular critic" by disguising the 1718 copies as a new edition.[8] Thereafter, despite much worthwhile writing and continued defenses by such people as Aaron Hill, Dennis's writings could not sell in large numbers.

Dennis was still writing into his seventies, publishing a translation of Thomas Burnet in 1730. But he was unable to continue work after that date. Several friends raised a hundred pounds for him by arranging a benefit performance of Vanbrugh's *The Provok'd Husband* on 18 December 1733. He died on 6 January 1734. The January 1734 number of the *Gentleman's Magazine* contains Hill's "Verses on the Death of Mr. Dennis," which focuses on a major strength of Dennis, his reasoning powers.

The earliest biography appears in Giles Jacob's *The Poetical Register* (1719). Because in the central critical reflections Jacob uses material sent him by Dennis, this early work contains none of Pope's anecdotal misrepresentations found in most later accounts. The anonymous 1734 *Life of Mr. John Dennis*—according to the title page "Not written by Mr. Curll" yet assembled in the very manner of that publisher's infamous literary lives—contains much old information and some independent conclusions. But this life and others published through the nineteenth century accept Pope's version of Dennis's character, maintaining the old anecdotes. Serious recasting of the image did not begin until 1888, with William Roberts's article in the *Dictionary of National Biography.* In our century many scholars have evaluated what Dennis actually did, not what Pope and other older sources said he was.

Chapter Two

General Literary Criticism

The Major Treatises

The Advancement and Reformation of Modern Poetry (1701) and *The Grounds of Criticism in Poetry* (1704) establish almost every major critical attitude found in Dennis's writings. When reading these two works, we may occasionally feel a point to be illustrated too far or an argument repeated too often, but such weaknesses actually point up a major virtue: Dennis is here creating something exciting. Having just piloted himself off the shallow waters of mere wittiness, as found in works like his burlesque poems, he now shoves off into waters new both to himself and to his readers. He proclaims in the epistle dedicatory of *The Advancement* "the Newness and Boldness of the Positions" that he will develop (*CW*, 1:197), and the title page of *The Grounds* promises "some New Discoveries never made before."

The Advancement and Reformation of Modern Poetry. Dennis had been working toward the thesis of *The Advancement* since the 1696 critique of Richard Blackmore's *Prince Arthur:* "Religion gives a very great Advantage for the exciting of Passion in Poetry" (*CW*, 1:198). Such a thought quickly draws him into several interesting lines of inquiry.

In part I Dennis offers his own answer to the old debate between Ancients and Moderns. Ancient poets have excelled modern writers because the ancients have usually chosen religious subjects. The proof lies mostly in a psychological sequence of logical steps. Passion is the chief element in poetry, and greater passion can be derived from a sacred subject than from a profane one, as seen in Homer, Milton, and Virgil. When the ancients write nonreligious poetry, they do not prove superior to the moderns. Furthermore, the Greeks' and Romans' greater poetry flourished and failed with their religion.

In part II Dennis argues "that the Moderns, by joining the

Christian Religion with Poetry, will have the Advantage of the Ancients" (*CW,* 1:278). His logic follows in two steps. First, the ends of Christianity (the true religion, in contrast to deism) and poetry are the same: to satisfy the reason, the passions, and the senses. Second, Christian poetry meets these three ends better than pagan poetry. Examples come from the Bible and Milton.

The essay proper seems to have a direct one-two structure, as if Dennis always knows exactly what he intends to say. But he is evidently mulling over what he has been writing, for the epistle dedicatory brings out implications or extensions of the essay. Most interestingly, he stresses the importance of rules and order in exciting the passions, noting that the seemingly irregular can have a definite place in order. Also notable is his hope that in modern times of deism and corruption, Christianity can strengthen the government and promote the public good.

The Grounds of Criticism in Poetry. Scholars have come to different conclusions about whether *The Advancement* or *The Grounds* is more important. Perhaps we should instead see the treatises as two stages in the rapid development of the writer's critical thought. *The Grounds* restates and amplifies many ideas found in *The Advancement,* so that there is a definite sense of repetition. At the same time, *The Grounds* assumes a new strength because the ideas are filled out more completely and are given a firm direction within a program designed to improve English literature.

In its published form, *The Grounds* is only a small part of an ambitious work that was to include also the rules for each poetic genre and biographies and critiques of selected English poets. As Hooker points out, this was the first English critical work published by subscription; unfortunately, positive response by only seventy-seven subscribers rendered it financially impossible to continue the project (*CW,* 1:507). Dennis by this time, of course, did not have the money to finance his own publication. Perhaps also he did not feel wholly confident about how to complete all the promised sections, because he was working within a vacuum—no English author had attempted this kind of project before. Compilers like Gerard Langbaine and William Winstanley had supplied capsulized summaries of authors' backgrounds and achievements, but no one had tried extensively to unite theory and individual evaluations. It would be very interesting to see how much further Dennis would have developed his general theories and how his authors' lives would have differed from Johnson's.

But as published, the fragmentary *Grounds* offers much of value. Dennis decries the current low esteem for true poetry and outlines his plan to help reestablish the noble art—he observes not too modestly that his design "is perhaps the greatest in this kind of Writing, that has been conceiv'd by the Moderns" (*CW,* 1:334). In chapters 2 through 4 he concentrates on the working of poetry; in chapter 5 he elaborates upon how modern authors can utilize religion to improve their poetry.

He defines poetry as an art by which the writer can excite passion to please and, more importantly, to reform our manners. The poet must rationally plan his composition, being sure especially to maintain order. Poetry divides into the greater poetry (which includes the epic, tragedy, and the greater ode) and the lesser poetry (which includes comedy, satire, elegy, pastoral, and the little ode)—the discussion on this point reads ambitiously albeit unclearly.

We can feel two kinds of passion, the vulgar and the enthusiastic. The enthusiastic passions, especially when raised by religious ideas, can lead to sublimity. The proof comes mostly from Longinus, Milton, Tasso, and Dennis's translation of the *Te Deum.*

The final chapter of *The Grounds* applies the general theory to the restoration of English literature, which, lacking religious inspiration, has become mostly a vain amusement. An interesting list of nine "Rules for employing Religion in Poetry" leads into two related concluding points: (1) not only is religion the basis of the greater poetry, but poetry is necessary to give force to religion, and (2) the reformation of poetry will benefit the public and all mankind.

Major Issues

As noted earlier, *The Advancement* and *The Grounds* bring up nearly all of Dennis's major critical ideas. To get a clearer conception of how he uses those ideas, we might briefly examine several of them more closely. We should consider the following:

order, the rules, passion, the sublime, and religion in literature.

In *The Grounds* Dennis establishes the Neoplatonic basis for
most of his work:

The Universe is regular in all its Parts, and it is to that exact Regularity
that it owes its admirable Beauty. The Microcosm owes the Beauty
and Health both of its Body and Soul to Order, and the Deformity
and Distempers of both to nothing but the want of Order. Man was
created, like the rest of the Creatures, regular, and as long as he
remain'd so, he continu'd happy; but as soon as he fell from his Primitive State, by transgressing Order, Weakness and Misery was the immediate Consequence of that universal Disorder that immediately
follow'd in his Conceptions, in his Passions and Actions.

The great Design of Arts is to restore the Decays that happen'd
to human Nature by the Fall, by restoring Order: The Design of
Logick is to bring back Order, and Rule, and Method to our Conceptions, the want of which causes most of our Ignorance, and all our
Errors. (*CW*, 1:335–36)

We cannot overemphasize the centrality of this viewpoint for
Dennis.

Firmly convinced of the macrocosm-microcosm analogy, he
sees everywhere signs of our Fall. Jugglers and Italian opera
singers performing before large audiences, theatrical factions
that keep sound plays off the stage, Alexander Pope's unjustified
success, widespread foreign luxuries, stock-jobbers' pernicious
influence upon a greedy public, Jacobite plotting against the
king, treacherous High Church priests—all indicate a radical
disorder throughout society.

To reestablish literary, social, and political order, we must
choose methods that themselves evince order. In literature, we
must insist upon rationality and regularity, upon methods and
forms that mirror the reason immanent in God's planning.[1]

In Neoclassical thought the reasonable way to establish literary order is to observe what Dennis terms "the Rules Deliverd
by Aristotle and His Interpreter Horace" (*CW*, 2:286). These
include for most Neoclassical critics such principles as overall
decorum of style and character; the three dramatic unities of
action, time, and place; the primacy of plot; the relative unimpor-
tance of spectacle; conventionalized character types; the role
of the chorus as an actor.

When insisted upon too mechanically and insensitively, as seen with Thomas Rymer and Charles Gildon, rules criticism deserves our censure. Indeed, major eighteenth-century authors easily expose such critics' weaknesses. Johnson in the *Preface to Shakespeare* destroys the case for the unities of time and place. In his *Battle of the Books,* Swift satirizes those moderns who focus on the means (the rules) rather than the ends of art. And the *Peri Bathous* ridicules the nonsensical urging of mechanical rules.

Dennis is sometimes castigated for his belief in the rules. He is taken as a hanging judge willing to formulate and impose the narrowest requirements on innocent literary victims. For example, William Godwin loathes this critic's "despotic pedantry" because "Dennis is indeed to the last degree a bigot in poetry. The rules of Aristotle (which are in reality nothing but the practice of the Greek poets drawn out into abstract maxims), the laws of the three unities, and the principle of what he calls 'poetical justice,' form the boundary of his conceptions, are his religion and his creed."[2]

Dennis, however, is actually quite moderate in his thinking about the rules. He argues, for instance, that too often "the Unity of Time is preserved by offending all Common Sense," while "the Unity of Place is preserv'd, sometimes by whimsical comick Absurdities, and sometimes by dreadful and prodigious Extravagancies." And he argues more generally that the greatest rule is to suspend a rule temporarily if in so doing the author can attain "Sovereign Beauty" (*CW,* 2:168–69, 198). The writer must develop the judgment to know when to observe or break the rules.

Dennis is assuming, of course, that the writer knows the rules before making such a decision. Ignorance only perpetuates that dreaded nonorder, for modern "Empiricks in Poetry" make the theaters "Mountebanks Stages, to treat *Aristotle* and *Horace* with as contemptuous arrogance, as our Medicinal Quacks do *Galen* . . . and to endeavour to make the Rules, that is, Nature and Right Reason, as ridiculous and contemptible as the Rules have made their Writings" (*CW,* 2:390).

As our critic writes in *The Causes of the Decay and Defects of Dramatick Poetry,* rules have validity because they are based on unchanging human nature. Careful analyses of reader or audience response within distinct genres have uncovered basic princi-

ples that produce successful works. Perhaps a Shakespeare can
disregard some principles because of his natural genius, but
most authors can only profit by such aid.

That Dennis goes well beyond rules alone can be seen in
his emphasis upon emotion in art. In fact, his greatest contribution to literary theory is his consistent argument for the centrality
of passion. He certainly leaves no doubt in *The Advancement:*
"Passion is the Characteristical Mark of Poetry, and therefore
it must be every where; for without Passion there can be no
Poetry" (*CW,* 1:215).

Dennis relies upon current psychology, as drawn from physical scientists like Harvey and Newton and such philosophers
as Aristotle, Plato, Descartes, Hobbes, and Locke.[3] One major
focus of this psychology is the sensitivity to the environment
that a creative artist must exercise. In particular, the artist will
experience strong passions, or feelings aroused in the soul by
large agitations of one's spirits.

But Dennis goes further than other critics in the central role
he gives passion. The more intense the passion felt by the writer,
he theorizes, the more intense the writing. Furthermore, passion
can be classified as two kinds. Ordinary passions, brought about
by causes known to the reader, include admiration, terror, and
joy. Enthusiastic passions, of more mysterious origin and aroused
upon reflection, are higher, more intense, more elevated—and
preferable in creating art.

Passion is not necessarily inimical to reason, as it often later
seems to be in the Romantic dichotomy between the two. Dennis
writes in defending the stage: "But then the Passions must be
rais'd after such a manner, as to take Reason along with them.
If Reason is quite overcome, the Pleasure is neither long, nor
sincere, nor safe." Or, in the context of poetry, we find that
"Poetry by the force of the Passion, instructs and reforms the
Reason" (*CW,* 1:150, 337). Over the years Dennis consistently
argues that we must not exalt reason over passion or passion
over reason, for each exalts the other. The result is a harmony
that brings us nearer the universal order.

The importance of strong feeling contributes much to Dennis's idea of sublimity. As early as 1688 he writes a friend about
crossing the Alps: ". . . the impending Rock that hung over
us, the dreadful Depth of the Precipice, and the Torrent that

roar'd at the bottom, gave us such a view as was altogether new and amazing. . . . we walk'd upon the very brink, in a litteral sense, of Destruction; one Stumble, and both Life and Carcass had been at once destroy'd. The sense of all this produc'd different motions in me, *viz.* a delightful Horrour, a terrible Joy, and at the same time, that I was infinitely pleas'd, I trembled" (*CW,* 2:380). He waxes still more eloquent as he climbs: "Ruins upon Ruins in monstrous Heaps, and Heaven and Earth confounded. The uncouth Rocks that were above us, Rocks that were void of all form, but what they had receiv'd from Ruine; the frightful view of the Precipices, and the foaming Waters that threw themselves headlong down them, made all such a Consort up for the Eye, as that sort of Musick does for the Ear, in which Horrour can be joyn'd with Harmony" (*CW,* 2:381).[4] At this early point Dennis has not yet the critical vocabulary to analyze his almost intuitive response of heightened emotion. He merely records his feelings, not using the words "sublime" or "passion."

But we soon find him referring to the unidentified Greek rhetorician "Longinus," who influenced English criticism after Boileau translated him in 1674. Longinus describes *hypsos,* which most English translations render as "sublimity" or "the sublime" and which refers to unusual, sustained elevation of conception and style. He devotes considerable space to the main sources of the sublime: the ability to form great conceptions, the stimulus of powerful and inspired passion, figurative language, noble diction, and the harmonious arrangement of words.[5]

Although Dennis finds the Greek treatise disappointingly remiss in not clearly defining the sublime, it obviously prompts him into his own definition. For him, the sublime consists in both a cause and its effects. The best poet worthily conveys his enthusiasm, "which is nothing but the Elevation, and Vehemence, and Fury proceeding from the Great, and Terrible, and Horrible Ideas." Such writing creates in the reader "Admiration and Surprize; a noble Pride, and a noble Vigour, an invincible Force, transporting the Soul from its ordinary Situation, and a Transport, and a Fulness of Joy mingled with Astonishment" (*CW,* 1:222–23).

Dennis offers and critically applies this kind of definition more than once, and always with considerable force, perhaps even enthusiasm. His excited repetition laid him open to the ridicule of the Scriblerus Club. He appears, for instance, as Sir Tremendous Longinus in *Three Hours after Marriage*. And Gay sarcastically dedicates to him *The Mohocks*—a farce offering madcap fustian and such characters as Gogmagog and Moonshine—because "the Subject of it is *Horrid* and *Tremendous*."[6] However, the critic's excitement really seems justified, for his new ideas about the sublime are exciting.

Samuel Johnson could not even tolerate the disquieting emotions aroused by religious poetry. Dennis, in contrast, relishes and cultivates such emotions. If sublimity involves power and elevation in both its subject matter and its effects upon the reader, it will be greatest where cause and effects are greatest. This neat logic is demonstrated for the enthusiastic passion of terror: "The greatest Enthusiastick Terror then must needs be deriv'd from Religious Ideas: for since the more their Objects are powerful, and likely to hurt, the greater Terror their Ideas produce; what can produce a greater Terror, than the Idea of an angry God?" (*CW*, 1:356). The same logic holds for the other enthusiastic passions.

Sublimity will be greatest in Christian poetry, as we see by again examining both cause and effects. For Christian poets, given the advantage of Revelation, "our Religion gives us more exalted Notions of the Power of an Infinite Being. . . . it consequently produces a stronger Spirit in Poetry, when it is managed by those who have Souls that are capable of expressing it." And in the reader "the Eye is ravishingly entertain'd, Admiration is rais'd to a Height, and the Reason is supremely satisfied. For are not these Effects that are worthy of an infinite Cause?" (*CW*, 1:271, 277).

In the Christian sublime, then, we can find literature of the greatest power and effectiveness. Using Christian material, the writer can combine passion, reason, and enthusiastic transport to give his readers supreme pleasure and insight into the universal world order.

We might briefly note how Dennis's Cambridge years may have affected his analysis of Christianity in art. His thinking is definitely Low Church, probably most greatly influenced by the Cambridge Neoplatonist tradition.[7] This we detect, for example, in his frequent reference to the microcosm-macrocosm correspondence. His whole system of viewing universal order depends, in fact, upon the validity of that correspondence. He also shares with the Cambridge Platonists a belief in reason as a way to move closer to God. At the same time, his psychology of the passions of the individual author and reader/audience places him within the tradition of English Protestant dissenters, which gave birth to the Cambridge Platonists.

Chapter Three

Evaluation of Fellow Authors

As tempted as we may be to focus on Dennis as a theorist, he never feels comfortable remaining with pure abstractions for any length of time. He always fills his literary criticism with reactions to other writers. *The Advancement* and *The Grounds,* for instance, are crammed with illustrative passages from authors whom he has studied closely in forming his generalizations.

Dennis finds some interesting things to say when he directly evaluates Milton and Shakespeare. He proves often still more interesting when he attacks literary opponents. He may viciously assail bitter personal enemies like Pope or Steele, counter a threat to the theater such as Jeremy Collier, or perhaps admonish an inept writer like Richard Blackmore. Whoever his target, he obviously enjoys throwing himself into the fray and seldom bores us.

Praise for Two Worthies

Milton. Dennis wrote the first significant extended criticism of Milton, whose *Paradise Lost* he declared "the greatest Poem that ever was written by Man" (*CW*, 1:351). This judgment he maintains in the preface to *The Passion of Byblis,* the *Remarks* on Blackmore, *The Advancement, The Grounds,* the *Remarks* on the *Dunciad,* the letters on Milton, and many other writings.

What made Milton "the first, who in the space of almost 4000 Years, resolved . . . to present the World with an Original Poem" (*CW*, 1:333)? It is his mastery of religious sublimity in poetry. In fact, Milton's lines comprise most of the illustrations of sublime poetry in both *The Advancement* and *The Grounds* (discussed in chapter 2). Dennis closely examines numerous illustrations to reveal "all that is great and sublime in Reason, express'd with the Spirit of that just Admiration, with which such worthy Thoughts of the Deity must naturally fill the Soul" (*CW*, 1:344). No one, he says, has written poetry greater than this.

But Dennis does not admire blindly, for he indeed points out faults in Milton. *Paradise Regained* cannot move him because of its weak spirit. Even *Paradise Lost* contains some flat passages. The most interesting weakness concerns Milton's machines, the angels in *Paradise Lost.* Unlike the gods and goddesses in classical poetry, these figures do not have the "manifest Bodies, and apparent humane Shapes, and the agreeable Distinction of Sexes" that make Greek and Roman works so delightful (*CW*, 2:229). With his usual honesty, Dennis has to think through his lack of sympathy with the nonhuman characters, a problem that has bothered later Milton critics.[1]

Throughout our century scholars have pleaded for wider recognition of Dennis's place in Miltonic criticism. He offers a close psychological examination of Milton's Christian sublimity, which can still be a useful approach. It is to Dennis's credit that Johnson, recognizing common sense, silently appropriated the remarks on Milton's epic machinery for the 1779 *Life of Milton.*[2]

Shakespeare. At the end of *The Impartial Critick* (1693), a parting blast at Thomas Rymer cryptically promises some extended discussion of the Bard: "But it does not follow, because *Shakespear* has Faults, that therefore he has no Beauties, as the next time we meet I shall shew you" (*CW*, 1:41). Although that promise was not kept until nearly twenty years later, different writings over his career indicate Dennis's continuing thought about Shakespeare.

Dennis makes use of Shakespeare in several ways. We find, for instance, incidental quotations from more than a dozen of the plays as Dennis argues various points. He can also use Shakespeare as a standard of excellence, as in his 25 May 1719 letter on degenerate public taste. Here we are told that as much as current playwrights and critics declare loudly against such Shakespearean weaknesses as rambling and too many plots, they cannot match or recognize his true characterizations, dialogue, and moving of passions (*OL*, 1:71–74). Of course, Dennis's adapta-

tions of *The Merry Wives of Windsor* and *Coriolanus* further attest
to his fascination with Shakespeare.

The critic's most valuable analysis of Shakespeare is *An Essay
on the Genius and Writings of Shakespear* (1712). Capitalizing
on the growing interest in Shakespearean criticism and the
chance to defend his own version of *Coriolanus,* Dennis writes
three letters developing a balanced view. He finds that Shakespeare possesses deep natural talent but fails to realize his full
potential because of his lack of education and the age in which
he lived.

Letter I outlines some advantages Shakespeare enjoyed from
birth, especially a bold imagination, the ability to create distin-
guishable characters and evoke terror, and a pure and diversified
expression. Unfortunately, his lack of art and learning makes
him commit gross errors with historical characters. For example,
Coriolanus and the Roman senator Menenius both act without
the dignity that historically they would have enjoyed. More
importantly, Shakespeare often fails to instruct us properly, because good and bad characters perish promiscuously. This failure
to observe poetic justice best illustrates his lack of art.

Letter II focuses on Shakespeare's unfamiliarity with Greek
and Latin writers. Because of this defect he lacks their art of
consistently harmonious designs and commits errors in historical
fact. His worst error is the totally mistaken characterization of
Julius Caesar, who should be portrayed gloriously.

In answer to the argument that someone able to write *The
Comedy of Errors* must have been able to read Plautus, Letter
III argues that Shakespeare probably could read Latin only with
difficulty. The main proof lies in his evidently not knowing
Horace, Sophocles, Euripides, or Terence, all of whom anyone
thoroughly acquainted with classical authors would cite. One
final problem is his not having time to consider and polish his
work.

Dennis is neither a thoughtless Bardolator nor a destructive
carper in this essay. Not only does he view Shakespeare as a
major genius of the world, but he counts himself one "who
loves and admires his Charms and makes them one of his chief
Delights, who sees him and reads him over and over and still
remains unsatiated . . ." (*CW,* 2:17). However, bringing out
Shakespeare's faults does two things: (1) we can more accurately
savor his great virtues, and (2) we can appreciate the alterations

that in Dennis's adaptation of *Coriolanus* will show Shakespeare to full advantage.

Although *An Essay on the Genius and Writings of Shakespear* deserves a place in Shakespearean scholarship, it does not seem a major document. Its most impressive strengths are the independence of its overall tone, the close scholarship concerning Shakespeare's learning, and its historical perspective. However, we do not sense the vigorous, full logic of *The Advancement.* Nor do we sense the great originality found, for example, in the author's reflections upon Milton. In particular, we find here none of the probing into the writer's inner workings that makes his analysis of Milton so much more significant.

The Defenses of the Stage

Jeremy Collier. Three of Dennis's more interesting pamphlets respond to attacks upon the theater by Jeremy Collier and William Law. Just after the Restoration a combination of social forces produced an explosion of antitheatrical sentiment and counterattack.[3] Foremost among the theater's critics was the clergyman Jeremy Collier, who advocated causes directly opposed to Dennis's.[4] Through numerous pamphlets, sermons, and political activities, Collier strove to discredit King William and the Revolution of 1688. The publication that first drew a response from Dennis is *A Short View of the Immorality, and Profaneness of the English Stage* (1698). Collier launches his attack along several lines: immodesty on the stage; profanity on the stage; abuse of the clergy in plays; playwrights' encouragement of immorality; flaws in plays by Dryden, John Vanbrugh, and other authors; the opposition of ancient and Church authorities to drama.

Writing in 1721, Dennis reflects upon his first reactions to the *Short View:* "It was towards the end of the last Century that Mr. *Collier* publish'd a Book call'd, *A short View of the Prophaness and Immorality of the* English *Stage;* in which Book, tho' there were several Things true in particular, yet the Author was manifestly so unfair an Adversary in general, that the latter End of the Book very grossly contradicted the beginning of it, and endeavour'd to decry even a Regulated Stage, which the Author at the beginning of the Book had acknowledg'd useful" (*OL,* 2:225). The result of his displeasure was *The Useful-*

ness of the Stage, to the Happiness of Mankind, to Government, and to Religion (1698).

He establishes in his introduction, much as he does in his 1721 recollection, a wholly reasonable focus:

> If Mr. *Collier* had only attack'd the Corruptions of the Stage, for my own Part, I should have been so far from blaming him, that I should have Publickly return'd him my Thanks: For the Abuses are so great, that there is a Necessity for the reforming them . . . ; the Corruptions of the Stage, hinder its Efficacy in the Reformation of Manners . . . , but when I found by his last Chapter, that his Design was against the Stage itself, I thought I could not spend a Month more usefully, than in the Vindication of it.
>
> My Business, therefore, is a Vindication of the Stage, and not of the Corruptions or the Abuses of it. (*CW*, 1:146–47)

A careful reading of the *Short View* reveals that Collier has indeed changed his focus in the last chapter, for the details in chapters 2 through 5 have no direct logical bearing on chapter 6. Thus Dennis can in effect concede the first chapters—elsewhere he does frequently assail the corruption of the popular audience's tastes—to concentrate on a question of central importance for critics since Plato.

The Usefulness of the Stage comprises three main parts: (I) the stage increases the happiness of people, especially the English; (II) the stage strengthens the government, especially in England; (III) the stage furthers the advancement of religion. Each part contains both positive proofs and refutations of objections raised by Collier and other like-minded disputants.

In part I Dennis develops an ingenious psychological argument: our chief end is happiness, which equals pleasure deriving from passion tempered by reason; such is the precise effect of well-written tragedy, which can also soothe painful passions. And how does this apply to the English? Here Dennis resorts to the psychosocial climatic theory of behavior: "Now, there is no Nation in *Europe* . . . that is so generally addicted to the Spleen, as the *English*. And . . . from the reigning Distemper of the Clime, which is inseparable from the Spleen, from that gloomy and sullen Temper, which is generally spread through the Nation; from that natural Discontentedness, which makes us so uneasy to one another, because we are so uneasy to ourselves . . ." (*CW,* 1:151). Thus the English need something to raise their passions. But at the same time their passions must move "agreeably to their Reasons." Therefore, they obviously need more drama. Dramatists did not produce the present corruption but only wrote to satisfy corrupted tastes; and "Poetry, Eloquence, History, and Philosophy, have appear'd, advanc'd, declin'd, and vanish'd with the Drama" (*CW,* 1:161).

Part II shows how tragedy helps rulers govern with strength and sensitivity and helps citizens purge wrongful passions and acknowledge their responsibilities. "Because there is no People on the Face of the Earth, so prone to Rebellion as the *English,* or so apt to quarrel among themselves," drama is especially necessary in England (*CW,* 1:167). In fact, in his attempt to see drama banned and in his other activities, Collier "has notoriously done all that lay in his little Power, to plunge us in another Civil War" (*CW,* 1:168). The refutation here is in the form of many examples proving that Collier has misread his authorities and does not understand how comedy rightly exposes follies in the great.

In part III Dennis advances an intricate argument that well-constructed tragedy in its handling of passion requires a belief in God and a future state; it also provides examples convincing us to perform our spiritual duties. Collier, meanwhile, shows ignorance of such basic dramatic principles as the need for characters' words to fit their nature (for instance, a vicious man should speak profanely) so that we may judge those characters properly. He also uses his older sources uncritically, not seeing, for example, that scripture condemns only idolatrous drama.

Dennis's pamphlet is the ablest reply to the *Short View.* As Hooker notes, "it is much more impressive than the replies of Congreve and Vanbrugh because it appears temperate and disinterested, because it discerns Collier's implications as well as his arguments, and because, instead of quibbling about the import of particular words, lines, or characters, it meets the fundamental issues by setting up a humanistic and reasonable philosophy of conduct" (*CW,* 1:467).[5] It is hard to see how anyone could more rationally bring out the arguments needed to disprove the *Short View.* Certainly, Dennis thought well of

The Usefulness of the Stage, since he included it in the 1721 *Original Letters* and the 1727 *Miscellaneous Tracts.* It was also pirated in 1738.

Some readers felt differently. The Middlesex Grand Jury indicted Dennis because he pronounced his countrymen prone to discontent (*CW,* 1:472), but the charge was quickly dropped; after all, the author's previous works display full support of the government, and *The Usefulness of the Stage* clearly continues that support. Harder to escape were the responses of Collier and his supporters. Arthur Bedford, for instance, hysterically accuses Dennis and others of "*Notorious Crimes,* destructive to *Christianity,* and tending to subvert the *Principles* of all *Religion,* and the *Notions* of *Good* and *Evil.*"[6] Bedford also finds much indecency in Dennis's *Gibraltar* and somehow manages to confuse him with Vanbrugh.

Collier himself responds more coolly and effectively in *A Defense of the Short View of the Profaneness and Immorality of the English Stage* (1699), a book designed to destroy the reputations of Congreve and Vanbrugh. Briefly giving us "a taste of Mr. *Dennis*'s Skill and Modesty," Collier argues that it is his opponent who misreads such authorities as the Bible.[7] We find similar objections to *The Usefulness of the Stage* in Collier's *A Second Defence of the Short View of the Prophaneness and Immorality of the English Stage* (1700).

These rebukes did not stir Dennis to a renewed attack; given the personal nastiness of many contemporary pamphlets, Collier seems gentle toward Dennis. However, events again pushed him into action after a terrible storm lashed England in November 1703. Many interpreted the storm as God's repayment to the nation for its sins.

One of the more influential of such arguments is *Mr. Collier's Dissuasive from the Play-House in a Letter to a Person of Quality Occasion'd by the Late Calamity of the Tempest* (1703). Here Collier repeats earlier points, but with a new emphasis upon God's manifest disapproval of the stage. During the week of the storm he even sees performances of *Macbeth* (with its witches' scenes) and *The Tempest* as acts of impiety flouting God's signs of anger. With the help of the Society for Promoting Christian Knowledge and other groups, the pamphlet was quickly distributed throughout churches and coffeehouses.

Dennis records the public response to Collier's newest work: ". . . it rais'd either the Indignation or Mirth of all discerning Men of Integrity. At the same time it had a wonderful Influence upon the Weak and the Hypocrites; and there was a great Outcry against the Stage; so great a one, that there was a warm Report about the Town . . . whether the Theatres should be shut up or continued. Then it was that I could bear no longer, but . . . I was resolved to expose the Hypocrisie, the Extravagance and the Sophistry of his *Dissuasive*" (*OL*, 2:226). His answer is *The Person of Quality's Answer to Mr. Collier's Letter, Being a Disswasive from the Play-House* (1704), purportedly written by one of Collier's stalwart champions. The pamphlet features three components: (1) the opening pages and two closing paragraphs, wherein the narrator doltishly condemns Collier while supposedly praising him; (2) his son Charles's strong direct attack on Collier; (3) his daughter Harriet's defense of the stage.

In the opening paragraphs the heavy-handed irony makes earnest jest of Collier's high regard for his tenets as the persona prays, "May he, for whose sake you did it, amply reward you" and laments that rats ("Play-House Vermin") have profanely chewed his copy of the *Short View* (*CW*, 1:299). He also unwittingly exposes Collier's fallacious logic, observing, for instance, that England's successful monarchs have supported the stage (*CW*, 1:300–303) and musing, "Not only the poor Inhabitants of *Cologn,* but the very *Hamburgers* and *Dantzickers,* and all the People of the *Baltick,* have suffer'd for the Enormities of our *English* Theatres; tho' I believe in my Conscience they never so much as heard of a Play, and know no more the Difference between a Tragedy and Comedy, than they do the Distance between the Earth and *Saturn*" (*CW*, 1:299–300).

The young Charles belligerently prods Collier with embarrassing questions such as why someone so interested in preserving the nation would not take the oath of allegiance and how this drama-hater has read so many plays. The more interesting Harriet, a spirited feminist, bluntly informs Collier that women are not so weak as to be easily corrupted by plays.

The Person of Quality's Answer provides some entertainment. It is, nonetheless, a relatively minor performance. Despite its saneness, we do not find here the close logical rigor of *The Usefulness of the Stage* or a concentration of new ideas. Not surprisingly, it prompted almost no comment upon either its original publication or its reprinting in the *Select Works*.

William Law. In 1726, the year of Collier's death, the mystic William Law aroused Dennis with *The Absolute Unlawfulness of the Stage-Entertainment Fully Demonstrated*. Law obviously has none of the playful spirit needed to enjoy the theater: "Any way of Life therefore that darkens our Minds, that misemploys our Reason, that fills us with a trifling Spirit, that disorders our Passions, that separates us from the Spirit of God, is the same certain Road to Destruction." Or, more specifically, "Let it therefore be observ'd, that the Stage is not here condemn'd, as some other Diversions, because they are dangerous, and likely to be Occasions of Sin; but that it is condemn'd, as Drunkenness and Lewdness, as Lying and Prophaneness are to be condemn'd . . . as such as are in their own Nature grossly Sinful."[8] The central problem, in Law's mind, is that enjoying a play is tantamount to worshiping images that re-create an impure world.

Law seems totally out of his element, for he takes his abstract proofs of theatrical sinfulness from other disputants, and he gives no hint whatsoever of knowing or having seen plays— in contrast to Collier and Bedford, who can squeeze two thousand examples into one pamphlet. Law's commentators agree that "it is decidedly the weakest of all his writings, and most of his admirers will regret that he ever published it."[9]

Dennis's rebuttal is *The Stage Defended, from Scripture, Reason, Experience, and the Common Sense of Mankind, for Two Thousand Years* (1726). He makes three main points: (1) Law evinces ignorance of scripture, of the nature of drama, and of "the present State of Religion, and Virtue, and Vice, among us" (*CW*, 2:305); (2) Law writes in an unchristian style; (3) drama strengthens the government. Most interesting is Dennis's thorough demonstration that Law badly misinterprets the biblical treatments of idolatry. Elsewhere, Dennis again borrows ideas from his own works. As Hooker notes, he obviously consulted his earlier stage defenses while composing the 1726 pamphlet (*CW*, 2:509).

The Stage Defended, then, seems derivative. But it is the most able refutation of Law. Instead of emotionally assailing "The Wild Rant, Blind Passion, and False Reasoning of that Piping-hot PHARISEE," as does one of Law's opponents,[10] Dennis hits directly upon Law's major logical weakness, clearly sets up his own positive points, and maintains a wholly reasonable tone. Indeed, as he reminds George Dodington in his prefatory letter, the author has an emotional stake in the welfare of English drama but can now write with no hope of personal profit, having "this Ten Years been obliged, by the most barbarous Treatment, to take Leave of the Playhouse for ever" (*CW,* 2:304). Although his final theatrical defense aroused little interest, it shows the aging Dennis still writing with the knowledge and strength of a worthy controversialist.

Thomas Rymer

In 1693 Dennis published his first work of literary controversy, *The Impartial Critick: or, Some Observations upon . . . A Short View of Tragedy.* Thomas Rymer's *A Short View of Tragedy* (1692), although confused in its overall structure, emphatically adheres to a commonsensical approach as the author consistently demands probability and decorum in tragedy. Troubled by weaknesses of modern English tragedy, Rymer suggests that dramatists return to Greek principles, such as use of the chorus; English tragedy might then realize its great potential. However, most readers now remember *A Short View of Tragedy* for its hostile criticism of works by Jonson and Shakespeare, especially *Othello,* which Rymer finds lacking in probability. In particular, Iago and other characters are not meted "poetical justice," a term coined by Rymer earlier in *Tragedies of the Last Age.*

In his introductory "A Letter to a Friend," Dennis asserts his intention to consider Rymer's proposed "Alterations in the Art of the Stage, which instead of reforming, would ruine the *English Drama*" (*CW,* 1:11). He reasons that, since the Greeks and the English have had greatly different climates, religions, and customs, it would be folly to reproduce Greek techniques on the English stage by reviving the chorus or declining to treat love onstage. The treatise itself consists of five dialogues between two young gallants, Jack Freeman and Ned Beaumont; this is Dennis's only critical work written in dialogue form. Through all the dialogues Freeman Socratically helps Beaumont learn through many questions and proofs.

In dialogue I Dennis moves slowly into a discussion of Rymer, who is found to err by writing criticism in an overly pleasant style rather than the proper "Didactick Style, [which] is a Stile that is fit for Instruction, and must be necessarily upon that account, pure, perspicuous, succinct, unaffected and grave" (*CW*, 1:16). Freeman in dialogue II finds Dryden and Nathaniel Lee's *Oedipus* inferior to that of Sophocles. Here Dennis in the main agrees with Rymer, except that our author goes on to praise Dryden's masterly ability to move us despite his technical mistakes. In dialogue III he examines Edmund Waller's "To the King on His Navy" line by line to disprove Rymer's contention that here English poetry found perfection, "that Not the language only, but His Poetry then distinguish'd him from all his contemporaries, both in *England* and in other Nations; And from all before him upwards to *Horace* and *Virgil*. For there, besides the Language Clean and Majestick, the Thoughts new, and noble; the Verse sweet, smooth, full and strong; the turn of the Poem is happy to Admiration."[11] Dialogues IV and V adapt Aristotle to counter Rymer's and Dacier's support for the chorus in modern tragedy.

We might quickly note two things that Dennis does not attempt to do. First, he does not refer directly to Rymer's attack on *Othello,* which comprises more than one-third of *A Short View of Tragedy.* As already noted, Freeman promises to expand upon Shakespeare's beauties "the next time we meet," but Dennis failed to fulfill this promise until he wrote his 1712 essay on Shakespeare. Charles Gildon, in *Miscellaneous Letters and Essays* (1694), wrote a derivative essay defending Shakespeare against Rymer's charges because Dennis had failed to deliver the promised rebuttal. Dennis, however, cannot in good conscience destroy Rymer's case against *Othello,* because he finds most of Rymer's censures against the Bard "very sensible and very just." As awkwardly or thoughtlessly as Rymer may at times bludgeon his target, Dennis shares his central view that a morally centered drama must observe some kind of poetic justice. Such a concept Dennis develops later, particularly in debating with Addison.

Second, he does not create a really unified treatise. He clearly establishes in the opening sentence of the introductory letter his focus upon Rymer's proposed theatrical reforms. But he also devotes many pages to Rymer's prose style and Waller's nondramatic poetry. Part of the explanation lies in the disunity of *A Short View of Tragedy* itself, which spins off a multitude of disparate topics, often in one- or two-sentence fragments. We also have in Dennis the give-and-take tempo of conversation and a wish to elaborate upon only a small number of Rymer's ideas.

Dennis at the same time accomplishes some interesting things in the book. Of prime importance are the Aristotelian analyses of audience response. Closely following Aristotle's "Interpreter *Dacier*," Dennis in dialogue II reasons, "For how can an Audience choose but tremble, when it sees a Man involv'd in the most deplorable Miseries, only for indulging those Passions and Frailties, which they are but too conscious that they neglect in themselves? And how can they choose but melt with compassion, when they see a Man afflicted by the avenging Gods with utmost severity, for Faults that were without malice, and which being in some measure to be found in themselves, may make them apprehensive of like Catastrophes?" (*CW,* 1:20). He takes Aristotle's notion of catharsis still further in dialogue IV: "For as the Humors in some distemper'd Body are rais'd, in order to the evacuating that which is redundant or peccant in them; so Tragedy excites Compassion and Terrour to the same end: For the Play being over, an Audience becomes serene again, and is less apt to be mov'd at the common Accidents of Life, after it has seen the deplorable Calamities of Hero's and Sovereign Princes" (*CW,* 1:33). And in dialogue V he refutes Dacier's arguments for the chorus by deftly adapting Aristotle's description of the entire tragic action; the properly designed sequence of beginning, middle, and end should ensure the audience of continuity between acts without resorting to the chorus. This early focus upon audience psychology clearly foreshadows Dennis's later theorizing about the significance of emotions in art.

The close reading of Waller demonstrates Dennis's interest in and mastery of technical verse theory (which doubtless made writing the 1722 "Of Prosody" no difficult task). He points out imperfections such as indecorously undignified words, obscure comparisons, unclear syntax, and noncontracted participles (for instance, "winged" for "wing'd"), which prove the poem under examination one of Waller's "most incorrect" works rather than "one of his rarest Masterpieces" (*CW,* 1:28). This relish for technical accuracy and supportive detail we find in most of Dennis's later writings, for this is how his mind functions.

Also characteristic is his independence in attacking a poet whom the age idolized in many tributes, including the hefty *Poems to the Memory of that Incomparable Poet Edmond Waller* (1688). In fact, one author, devastated upon reading the criticism, demands, "And you, audacious Mortal, tell me why / You dare my Fav'rite *Waller's* Faults descry?"[12]

In the pages on Waller and elsewhere in the book, Dennis is indeed the "impartial critic." Rymer could not achieve impartiality about Waller, since he not only contributed three fulsome poems to the 1688 collection of Waller elegies but also put the epitaph on the poet's tomb. Dennis, in contrast, more than once balances his technical censure with admiration: "I have always admir'd Mr. *Waller,* for a great Genius, and a gallant Writer. Nor am I more pleas'd with any of his Excellencies, than with the clearness of his happy turns" (*CW,* 1:25). As in the 1712 letters on Shakespeare, Dennis's intellectual honesty will let him play neither the idolator nor the pure carper. And several times in other dialogues he explicitly tells us that Rymer is right on many points. Nor does he ever hurl diatribes at the man. It is no wonder that the January 1693 *Gentleman's Journal* compliments Rymer's "ingenious Adversary, if we may stile him an Adversary, who hath answer'd him with all imaginable civility." We might wish that Dennis had exercised such balance and self-restraint in his anti-Pope writings.

The Impartial Critick seems designed to show Dryden and the rest of the literary world what its author can do as a critic. He chooses and develops a limited number of concepts with which he establishes his credentials as literary scholar, critical theorist, independent thinker, and prose stylist. The strong contrast between the witty, sometimes off-color tone of the transitional banter of the two friends and the complete seriousness when the conversation turns to literature suggests an author ready to leave behind mere wittiness for solid critical work. Indeed, *The Impartial Critick* is an impressive first critical treatise, as acknowledged by J. E. Spingarn, who includes it in his *Critical Essays of the Seventeenth Century,* and Marvin Herrick, who finds it "the most sensible of the long array of critical writings from Dennis' pen."[13]

Richard Blackmore

The physician-poet Richard Blackmore in 1695 published *Prince Arthur. An Heroick Poem,* a Christian epic with a mythical British setting. Although by modern standards awkwardly didactic, verbose, metrically unvaried, and often pretentiously Miltonic, the book reached its fourth edition by 1697. Dennis, seeking a way to extend his reputation as a critic, which had been developing since *The Impartial Critick,* seized upon the chance by publishing *Remarks on a Book Entituled, Prince Arthur* (1696).

The preface makes clear that what we have of the *Remarks on . . . Prince Arthur* is perhaps one-half of a planned whole, which would also include discussions of poetic expression and poetic genius, briefly defined here as "the expression of a Furious Joy, or Pride, or Astonishment, or all of them caused by the conception of an extraordinary hint" (*CW,* 1:47). The essay itself consists of two parts, each eight chapters long. It demonstrates the lack of merit in *Prince Arthur* by systematically developing and applying the terms in an Aristotelian definition of epic taken directly from René Le Bossu: "An Epick Poem is a Discourse invented with Art, to form the Manners by Instructions disguis'd under the Allegory of Action, which is important, and which is related in Verse in a delightfull, probable and wonderfull manner" (*CW,* 1:55). Extensive contrasts between *Prince Arthur* and Virgil's *Aeneid* highlight Blackmore's artistic inferiority.

Part I treats the first two-thirds of Le Bossu's definition. The action of an epic poem combines with its moral to make up the fable, writes Dennis. The author must create unity of action, not a medley of irregular episodes. Blackmore fails in "that his Action is not one, and that it is not Entire, nor Universal, nor Allegorical; and consequently, that his Poem is no Fable, and no Heroick Poem" (*CW,* 1:69).

In part II Dennis shows that Blackmore does not write "in a delightfull, probable and wonderfull manner." A major failing lies in the inconsistency of the poet's characters. To demonstrate proper treatment of a character's manners, Dennis rewrites a scene from Euripides' *Hippolytus.* Finally, the incidents in *Prince Arthur* do not produce delight, because they are not agreeable in their nature (especially when they involve Christian machinery, that is, "the divine and infernal Persons"), are insufficient in number or variety, and are not surprising or pathetic.

In discussing *Prince Arthur,* Dennis clearly defends the Neoclassical ideals of unity and order. The most interesting point here is the demand for consistent manners in each character. Arthur himself seems at first pious and valorous, but he shamefully neglects his people after they have been wearied and dispirited by a storm. Virgil, in contrast, expertly creates an Aeneas consistently fearless, pious, and transcendently good. The insistence upon such characterization becomes a significant feature of Dennis's plays, especially *Rinaldo and Armida,* where he changes Tasso's characters drastically to achieve a consistency that he feels necessary in tragedy.

In demanding unity, Dennis by no means discounts emotion. "Poetical Genius," he insists, ". . . is it self a Passion. A Poet then is oblig'd always to speak to the Heart." Part of Blackmore's failure lies in his not realizing how "Compassion charms us, and Terrour shakes us, and both of them very much please us" (*CW,* 1:127). The critic's extended analysis of Aristotle's thoughts on passion and of Virgil's and Blackmore's disparate abilities to arouse passion concludes his *Remarks on . . . Prince Arthur* strongly. Passion is clearly assuming a major place in his aesthetic, as we find again shortly in *The Advancement.*

Formal perfection and strong emotion work together "to demonstrate the Moral" in an epic composed with Virgil's skill. Blackmore, lacking both technical expertise and genius, cannot deliver any kind of moral; instead he merely assembles a disjointed sequence of incidents. Dennis's firm insistence upon the central moral later assumes various guises. We see it in his support of poetic justice, the didactic focus of his own serious drama, and his defenses of the theater. In his mind, literature is no mechanical exercise but a significant force toward our moral well-being.

We must remember that Dennis does not intend to ridicule either Blackmore or his poetry. He writes in his dedication, "I believe *Prince Arthur* to be neither Admirable nor Contemptible. For if I had the one or the other Opinion, I should certainly never have Written against him."[14] Such a balanced tone leads Aaron Hill in the 25 September 1724 *Plain Dealer* to commend the "just, and generous Reprehension" in the *Remarks on . . . Prince Arthur.*

Actually, analysis of *Prince Arthur* is here no more than a subsidiary aim. Dennis's central intent seems more ambitious. He brings together Blackmore's epic and the *Aeneid* in order to progress toward a definition of a closely worked out critical system. Although he apologizes for writing hastily, the care with which he develops his system is seen in the painstaking movement from point to point as he amplifies his definition of epic. We read, for instance: "The Incidents in *Prince Arthur* are not delightfull, for the following Reasons. First, because they are not in their Natures agreeable. Secondly. . . ." His six-reason list completed, he proceeds to explore each in turn: "First, The Incidents are not in their Natures agreeable. The things included in Mr. *Blackmore*'s Narration are chiefly four: Voyages, Wars, Councils, Machines. Now there are three things that make a Voyage delightfull to the Reader. 1. The interest that he has in the Person that takes it . . ." (*CW,* 1:103). This densely layered style, if slow reading at times, reinforces Dennis's statements in the preface about the high importance of a critic's "Design to contribute that little which lies in his power to advance the Art upon which he makes his Reflections" (*CW,* 1:49).

The *Remarks on . . . Prince Arthur* shows Dennis successfully beginning to establish a coherent, unified approach to criticism. It introduces several critical ideas that he clarifies and extends in later works. Furthermore, the book succeeds within "the best tradition of the neoclassical approach to the epic—a combination of established theory, good sense, and critical perspicacity."[15]

The attack on *Prince Arthur* did not lead to a full-fledged quarrel between the two writers. The prologue to our author's *A Plot, and No Plot* (1697) does jest about Blackmore's vaunted composition of verses while riding in his coach, but this prologue was written by someone else and was not reprinted in the 1718 version of the play included in *The Select Works.* In *A Satyr against Wit* (1700), Blackmore only briefly sandwiches Dennis in among the "*Mob* of Wits" assailed for their bantering emptiness. "To the Cheapside Knight, on his Satyr against Wit," published in *Commendatory Verses on the Author of the Two Arthurs and the Satyr against Wit* (1700), has long been ascribed to Dennis. Its points against Blackmore, however, bear no resemblance to those made in the *Remarks on . . . Prince Arthur.* If it is indeed Dennis's, he shows no venom; in fact, the awkward jibes in its thirteen lines strike us only for their lackluster quality.

Indeed, Blackmore and Dennis soon found themselves on close terms. We find Blackmore's name in the 1704 subscription list for Dennis's projected critical magnum opus. Between 1716 and 1720 the two men correspond several times. And Dennis's *Original Letters* (1721), significantly, both begins and ends with letters to Blackmore.

While neither ever totally gives way in his opinions (Blackmore, for instance, continues to favor Christian machinery), we find them agreeing on many major points. A 1716 letter from Dennis, in fact, lists fourteen tenets that they share. Most important is the mutual insistence "that the Fable and the Action must be only for the Moral" (*OL,* 1:2). Not surprisingly, Dennis makes Blackmore his prime recipient of letters outlining the place of Christianity in a healthy state. Meanwhile, in the preface to *Alfred* (1723), Blackmore commends Dennis for promoting Christianity.

We must admire the sensibleness of these two writers, who finally come to emphasize their shared fundamental assumptions more than their disagreements on relatively minor technical questions.

Joseph Addison

Dennis enjoyed a relationship with Joseph Addison that combined personal respect and fruitful disagreement. On many important topics they fully agreed. For example, both embraced Whig doctrines, enjoying the patronage of the Earl of Halifax and receiving substantial rewards for their poetic celebrations of the great Whig hero the Duke of Marlborough. Addison, like Dennis, wrote admiringly of Milton. He likewise concurred in Dennis's firm insistence that the writer can help reform the nation's morals, as he makes clear in *Rosamond, Cato,* and many *Spectator* papers.[16]

Real controversy developed between the two men only between 1711 and 1713. The causes of disagreement were two.

First, several papers in the *Spectator* and the *Tatler* had attacked critics in general, some of Dennis's favorite critical theories, and, Dennis thought, Dennis himself. In a 1713 letter to the Duke of Buckingham, he expresses a willingness to disbelieve Addison's share in the authorship of the offending papers, "but he was in Partnership with those who did [that is, Steele]. He went share in the Profits, and more than Share in the Reputation" (*CW*, 2:399). Second, he honestly believed that Addison's *Cato* did not merit the hysterical popular adulation that it received.

We can easily feel the lack of personal animosity between the men. For his part, Addison strongly disapproved of Pope's brutal pamphlet against Dennis, *The Narrative of Dr. Robert Norris* (1713), and he subscribed to Dennis's *Select Works*. Dennis, in turn, admired Addison's Milton criticism, and he wrote in the preface to *Original Letters*, "I think my self oblig'd to do Justice to the Memory of Mr. ADDISON, who was certainly a Learned and very Ingenious Man: And several of the *Tatlers* and *Spectators* which were writ by him deserv'd the Applause which they met with" (*CW*, 2:415).

The two most interesting points of debate between Addison and Dennis concern poetic justice and *Cato*. Dennis had for some time argued for dramatists' as far as possible meting out to characters fortunes determined by their moral conduct. His logic derives from his central position that the moral and the fable must reinforce within us a proper sense of God's universal order. He argues in *The Usefulness of the Stage,* for example, that poetic justice is

an Image of the Divine, and [it thus supposes] the Being of a God and Providence. It supposes too the Immortality of the Soul, and future Rewards and Punishments. For the Things which in perfect Tragedy bring Men into fatal Calamities, are involuntary Faults; that is, Faults occasion'd by great Passions. Now this upon a Supposition of a future State, is very just and reasonable. For since Passions in their Excesses, are the Causes of most of the Disturbances that happen in the World, upon a Supposition of a future State, nothing can be more just, than that the Power which governs the World, should make sometimes very severe Examples of those who indulge their Passions; Providence seems to require this. (*CW*, 1:183)

We can easily see why he feels a new version of *Coriolanus* necessary: "The Good must never fail to prosper, and the Bad must be always punish'd: Otherwise the Incidents, and particularly the Catastrophe which is the grand Incident, are liable to be imputed rather to Chance, than to Almighty Conduct and to Sovereign Justice. The want of this impartial Distribution of Justice makes the *Coriolanus* of *Shakespear* to be without Moral" (*CW*, 2:6).

Against this doctrine Addison directed *Spectator* 40 (16 April 1711). The paper opens with a telling passage:

The *English* Writers of Tragedy are possessed with a Notion, that when they represent a virtuous or innocent Person in Distress, they ought not to leave him till they have delivered him out of his Troubles, or made him triumph over his Enemies. This Errour they have been led into by a ridiculous Doctrine in modern Criticism, that they are obliged to an equal Distribution of Rewards and Punishments, and an impartial Execution of poetical Justice. Who were the first that established this Rule I know not; but I am sure it has no Foundation in Nature, in Reason, or in the Practice of the Ancients. We find that Good and Evil happen alike to all Men on this Side the Grave; and as the principal Design of Tragedy is to raise Commiseration and Terrour in the Minds of the Audience, we shall defeat this great End, if we always make Virtue and Innocence happy and successful. Whatever Crosses and Disappointments a good Man suffers in the Body of the Tragedy, they will make but small Impression on our Minds, when we know that in the last Act he is to arrive at the End of his Wishes and Desires.[17]

He goes on to observe that good tragedies, including most of Dryden's, have indeed been constructed by the poetic justice formula. However, the many fine tragedies written otherwise, including *Othello* and *King Lear,* prove that tragedians do not have to employ poetic justice.

Dennis's response takes the form of a letter, "To the Spectator, upon His Paper on the 16th of April," first published with *An Essay on the Genius and Writings of Shakespear* (1712). The letter in its early paragraphs seems rather snappish—his opposition is labeled "insolent," "dogmatick," "deluded," "dictatorian"—because he believes Steele to be the author of the offending *Spectator* essay. It settles down, however, to aesthetic argument and valuable reformulation of Dennis's logic.

He does not find convincing Addison's proof based on what we see in the world outside the play. He argues that "Good and Evil does not happen alike to all Men on this side the Grave." It seems only just that Providence should punish us for indulging our passions; however, we cannot know what passions lurk within others, since the virtuous command their passions and the wicked dissemble and conceal theirs. Thus we cannot know whether another person deserves his fate, as we can for a poetic creation.

The analysis proceeds: "But suppose I should grant that there is not always an equal Distribution of Affliction and Happiness here below. Man is a Creature who was created immortal, and a Creature consequently that will find a Compensation in Futurity for any seeming Inequality in his Destiny here. But the Creatures of a poetical Creator are imaginary and transitory; they have no longer Duration than the Representation of their respective Fables; and consequently, if they offend, they must be punish'd during that Representation" (*CW*, 2:20–21). The theatrical poetic justice figures, then, as "a very narrow and a very imperfect Type" of God's ultimate distribution of rewards and punishments.

Extra support derives from reinterpretation of Aristotle's thinking on proper tragic heroes. Dennis brings his idea of passions into Aristotle's definition:

> We are neither to make them very virtuous Persons on the one side, that is Persons who absolutely command their Passions, nor on the other side Villains who are actuated by inveterate Malice, but something between these two, that is to say Persons who neglecting their Passions suffer them to grow outragious, and to hurry them to Actions which they otherwise would abhor. And that Philosopher expressly declares . . . that to make a virtuous Man unhappy, that is a Man who absolutely commands his Passions, would create Horror instead of Compassion, and would be detested by all the World. And thus we have shewn that *Aristotle* is for Poetical Justice. . . . (*CW*, 2:21)

Furthermore, since Aristotle is basing his observations upon the plays of Sophocles and Euripides, those dramatists must be practicing poetic justice.

Dennis is making a readable and, on the whole, sound exposition of poetic justice stemming from his belief in the exemplary function of a drama imitating ideal nature, but he does not exactly refute Addison, who focuses instead on audience response within this empirical world. Indeed, Addison in *Spectator* 548 (28 November 1712) declares "that the Instruction and Moral are much finer, where a Man who is virtuous in the main of his Character falls into Distress, and sinks under the Blows of Fortune at the end of a Tragedy, than when he is represented as Happy and Triumphant. Such an Example corrects the Insolence of Human Nature, softens the Mind of the Beholder with Sentiments of Pity and Compassion, comforts him under his own private Affliction. . . ."[18]

Addison's thoughts on poetic justice have much to do with his tragedy *Cato* (1713), in which the highly noble Cato commits suicide. The play enjoyed a tumultuously positive reception: Whigs and Tories alike clamored to applaud it, especially for its celebration of liberty; complimentary poems and treatises flew off the presses; the play went into several English editions in 1713; foreign readers came to know it quickly in translations. Such success, coupled with the sureness that *Cato* violated several major dramatic principles, pushed Dennis into a response.

Thus in 1713 Dennis published *Remarks upon Cato, a Tragedy.* The introduction of this pamphlet early points up his distress at "the general and the violent Applause" for *Cato.* He complains about the encomia, particularly *Cato Examin'd* (which praises *Cato* for closely observing the dramatic rules). True to the stronger elements of his own personality, he also stoutly proclaims his resolution to think independently. Given his strong emotions about Addison's play, as outlined in the introduction, Dennis in the *Remarks* themselves writes with admirable restraint and keen insight. He attempts here to demonstrate the weaknesses of *Cato* in light of the Aristotelian rules.

Addison, he notes, encounters problems, first, with structure. His play has no fable, "since there can be no Fable, where the Action is neither Allegorical nor Universal; and the Action in this Tragedy of *Cato,* is neither Allegorical nor Universal; I appeal to the Impartial Reader, whether this Tragedy of *Cato* having no Fable, can justly be said to be a fine Tragedy." With no fable, of course, a play signifies nothing. At the same time, numerous incidents in the play "not only corrupt its Unity, but render it improbable, Romantick and incredible" (*CW*, 2:46–47).

Dennis finds that such mishandling of the basic structure makes it impossible for us to feel compassion or terror. In an extremely rare kind of personal glimpse, he illustrates how he himself reacts as a spectator:

I sit with Indolence from the opening of the Play to the very Catastrophe; and when at length the Catastrophe comes, instead of vehemently shaking with Terror, or dissolving with melting Pity, I rather burn with Indignation, and I shudder with Horror. When I beheld *Cato* expiring by his own Hand, 'tis difficult to tell at which Indecency and which Inconsistency I am shock'd the most, at a Philosopher's acting against the Light of Nature, or at a *Stoick*'s yielding to ill Fortune without the last Necessity, or at the unjust and unfortunate End of a Man of accomplish'd Virtue, or at a Lover of Liberty and of his Country deserting both by his Death. (*CW*, 2:47)

As might be expected, Dennis cannot accept Addison's failure to create "an exact Distribution of a Poetical Justice" (*CW*, 2:49). We learn here nothing new about his concept of poetic justice, but he clearly demonstrates how Cato's demise violates the doctrine. This and other problems combine, for him, to make the dramatic effect improbable rather than wonderful.

We find even more insight in the analysis of Addison's characters. Cato, for example, displays three qualities that make him a poor tragic hero: (1) he acts too virtuously to arouse either pity or terror; (2) his behavior does not remain consistent from one act to another; (3) above all, he is a Stoic and

therefore an improper Heroe for Tragedy, not because he is suppos'd to be actually without Passion, but because he is believ'd to do his utmost Endeavours to be without them; because he places his Pride, his Glory, his Excellence in subduing them; because his great and principal Aim is to make his Reason, not only the Ruler, but the very Tyrant of them; because his chief Design is not to regulate, but to extirpate and extinguish them. . . . his Philosophy has taught him to check his Passions, to conceal them, and to shorten them; so that a *Stoick* . . . can never be shewn, as *Oedipus* and some other

principal Characters of Tragedy are shewn, *viz.* agitated and tormented
by various violent Passions, from the opening of the Scene to the
very Catastrophe. (*CW,* 2:50)

In this argument Dennis combines his long-standing concern
about the relation between reason and passion in art with his
gift for pursuing terms of a definition to elucidate a very real
weakness in Addison's conception of his tragic hero.

The other characters in the play likewise show a flawed dramatic craft on Addison's part. For instance, in contrast to Cato,
Sempronius and Syphax act too wickedly to arouse a tragic response. Overall, the dramatis personae all act too inconsistently
and unnaturally for us to feel any kind of tragic emotion.

Dennis notes many ways in which Addison devises incidents
that prove unreasonable and unmoving. The most interesting
such fault is the playwright's unthinking observation of the dramatic rules. Dennis explains the problem in one of the most
memorable paragraphs of the pamphlet:

We have hitherto shewn the Faults that this Author has committed
for want of observing the Rules. We shall now shew the Absurdities
with which he abounds thro' a too nice observing some of them,
without any manner of Judgment or Discretion. The Unities of Time
and Place are mechanick Rules, which, if they are observ'd with Judgment, strengthen the reasonableness of the Incidents, heighten the
probability of the Action, promote the agreeable Deceit of the Representation, and add Cleanliness, Grace, and Comeliness to it. But if
they are practis'd without Discretion, they render the Action more
improbable, and the Representation more absurd, as an unworthy
Performance turns an Act of the highest Devotion into an Act of
the greatest Sin. (*CW* 2:68)

He then displays considerable acumen and forcefulness as he
closely examines numerous passages illustrating this weakness.

Remarks upon Cato makes good reading, in no small part because Dennis here writes with verve. He ridicules Addison's
inconsistencies with such sentences as "If this is Tragical, I would
fain know what is Comical" or "Now how a Man could fight
and fall with his Face muffled up in his Garment, is, I think, a
little hard to conceive" (*CW,* 2:78). More importantly, as much

as the contemporary audience responded to the symbolism within *Cato,* Dennis can often strike us as right in his strictures.[19] Addison has not written a totally satisfying play, and the critic gives some valid reasons why. In particular, *Cato* does seem rife with improbabilities, and the characters do fail to arouse strong emotion. Dennis's judgment met the thorough approval of no less a critic than Johnson, who in his life of Addison not only commends Dennis but quotes a dozen passages from *Remarks upon Cato* (*CW,* 2:448).

The 1713 pamphlet concentrates on "the absurd Conduct of the Tragedy of *Cato*" (*CW,* 2:81). Between 1713 and 1718 Dennis composed two long letters focusing on the sentiments of the play, but through some unidentified chicanery, as we learn particularly in the preface to the *Original Letters,* both the originals and the copies were stolen or misplaced. Dennis then recast his thoughts in the form of seven brief "Letters upon the Sentiments of the Two First Acts of *Cato,*" which he published in the *Original Letters.*

The seven letters belittle several absurdities. Frequent exclamations about the long-ago battle at Pharsalia rather than about the recent one at Thapsus, Stoics' nonstoic speeches, Sempronius's dullness and stupidity, the wrongly praised scene in which "*Syphax* is very much in the wrong in his Invectives against the *Romans,* [and] *Juba* is more in the wrong in his Defence of them" (*CW,* 2:86), Juba's mistimed declaration of passion for Marcia, the unreasonable proposals made in the Roman Senate—these and other problems convince Dennis of the total unworthiness of the sentiments. Granted, many of his observations reveal close reading of troublesome passages. However, the critical remarks read more like quibbles than like the significant questions pursued in *Remarks upon Cato.* Thus the letters add little of substance to Dennis's criticism of Addison.

Fortunately, Dennis and Addison never descended to the bitter enmity that perverted the relationships Dennis suffered with Steele and Pope. Addison subscribed to Dennis's *Select Works,* while in the preface to the *Original Letters* Dennis praises Addison. Finally, even in the minor letters upon *Cato,* Dennis exhibits the intellectual power to pursue a critical thesis with a hunger for rigorous detail befitting the sort of critic he was always longing to be.

Richard Steele

We find much waste of critical energy in three publications directed mainly against Richard Steele and published between 1720 and 1723. The two men shared views held by many Whigs since the Revolution: Steele's political pamphlets, essays, and poetry argue that William III "is the Hope and Stay of *Europe*," Marlborough is the "wonderful Instrument of Providence," the clergy must not revile others, and the Hanoverian Succession may preserve the nation.[20] Both enjoyed the patronage of such influential Whigs as Godolphin and Halifax. Agreeing on Blackmore's artistic banality, both contributed to the *Commendatory Verses*. Both stressed public service for the national good, one aspect of which was reformation of the stage. And early in their relations Dennis read for Steele and Addison manuscripts of *The Battle of Ramillia* and other writings.

However, by 1710 relations were fraying. A 28 July letter from Dennis to Steele complains that his old friend Captain Steele has "departed, and some Gentleman has succeeded him in the old House, with the same Name, and the same Martial Title." A 1714 letter to Walter West similarly accuses Steele of brutality and contemptuousness (*OL,* 1:28, 2:287–88). From then on, as Dennis's affairs grew steadily more desperate while his old friend's prospered, the relationship never could return to its former state, even during the years that the two men made peace or at least suspended hostilities.

A fierce explosion erupted in connection with theatrical affairs between 1718 and 1720. In 1718 Steele, now patentee, or governor, at Drury Lane, along with his actor-managers Colley Cibber, Barton Booth, and Robert Wilks, was vigorously opposing the Lord Chamberlain's demand for closer governmental supervision of theaters. Steele invited Dennis to read *The Invader of His Country* before Cibber, Booth, and himself.

The Drury Lane management agreed to produce the play, but, unfortunately, the production suffered numerous delays and in 1719 failed on the stage. We learn Dennis's version of what happened from the bitter dedication addressed to the Lord Chamberlain and from two frantic although not wholly vituperative letters written in March and April 1719 (*CW,* 2:176–80, 162–67). He accuses the actor-managers ("two or three Insolent

Players") of at first applauding the work but then so contriving delays that *The Invader of His Country* had to face impossible competition, including the king's arrival in London. Matters did in fact become so tense that Cibber had Mrs. Oldfield speak an epilogue for *The Invader of His Country* viciously assailing the play!

In *The State of the Case between the Lord-Chamberlain and the Governor of the Royal Company of Comedians* and his periodical the *Theatre* (both 1720), Steele, writing as "John Edgar," praises the current prosperity of British drama. He defends particularly the great contribution of actors to the success—and he includes here the actor–managers' wise handling of daily theatrical affairs. But having just seen these actor–managers destroy his play (as he viewed the problem), Dennis felt no inclination to agree with Steele. Thus he published in early 1720 two letters entitled *The Characters and Conduct of Sir John Edgar, Call'd by Himself Sole Monarch of the Stage in Drury-Lane; and His Three Deputy-Governors.* Third and fourth letters were issued approximately one month later. The wish to refute Steele permeates the letters: "The Intention of your Paper, call'd *The Theatre,* is most apparently to support, in Defiance of the Court and Town, a Parcel of impudent Players, in Pride, Presumption, Folly, Ignorance, Insolence" (*CW,* 2:193).[21]

Letter I, in part a repetition of some earlier letters, briskly attacks actors, Cibber, and Steele. Dennis finds dramatic art dying because of control by actors lacking education, seeking monetary gain, and bearing two thousand years of low reputation. Cibber, characterized by impiety, dissoluteness, disregard for social and familial values, and intellectual imposture, has "neither Wit by Nature, nor Learning by Education" (*CW,* 2:188). Steele actually receives less harsh treatment here than does Cibber. The criticism of Steele is mostly *ad hominem,* for his low beginnings, financial losses on silly projects such as a mechanical petticoat, plagiarism, and packing audiences with his friends.

Letter II concerns itself much more with aesthetic questions, somewhat less with personalities. Dennis focuses mainly upon Steele's disapproval in the *Theatre* of the dramatic rules, especially the unities. He brings in the authority particularly of Jonson to argue that rules are indeed of major importance, although one can suspend them when necessary. In passing, he labels Steele and the actor–managers mountebanks, interestingly ranking them with Henry Sacheverell, "a grave Divine turn[ed] Mountebank" whom Dennis had battled in 1702.

The first part of *The Characters and Conduct* gained a large immediate readership, a second edition appearing within the same year. Steele himself, *"The injur'd Knight,"* attests to its popularity when in the 6 February issue of the *Theatre* he attacks this pamphlet "yesterday put into my Hands by an Hawker." His heart seems barely in his effort, however, for he addresses none of Dennis's substantive points. He does much better in his 9 February issue, wherein he assails critics—particularly Dennis—for their abuse of real writers. He vividly groups Dennis with "Otters, Polecats, Foxes, Kites, and Scriech–Owls . . . whom, from the Obscenity of their Make, and Reptility of their Being, [Nature] has appointed to shun the Day. . . ."[22]

The third and fourth letters of *The Characters and Conduct,* responses to the two issues of the *Theatre* just quoted, fully convey Dennis's outrage. Steele now becomes the sole target, *ad hominem* argument and turning of the tables become the major techniques, and the style becomes viciously aggressive.

Letter III basically concentrates on Steele's moral character. He is seen not as he sees himself, the clearheaded judge of the *Theatre,* but as an ugly, ignorant coward guilty of dishonesty and fettered with legal problems, including indebtedness to Dennis. Above all, he is "an illiterate Pedant . . . the very Cock Pedant of all the Nest of Pedants" with "a dogmatizing Spirit, a presumptuous Arrogance, and a soaring Insolence" (*CW,* 2:204, 203). Much the same spirit continues in the final letter. The only real critical observation in this letter has Dennis agreeing with his opponent that the stupidest writers become critics; but the direction of the accusation reverses against Steele when he is set up as the best example of this generalization. The writing is again peppery and brisk, especially in the vivid concluding "Picture of Sir *John Edgar*" countering Steele's satiric portrait of Dennis. Dennis's hatred seethes through the specific description of Sir John's "middle Stature, broad Shoulders, thick Legs, a Shape like the Picture of *somebody* over a Farmers Chimney, a short Chin, a short Nose, a short Forehead, a broad flat Face, and a dusky Countenance" (*CW,* 2:213).

Although *The Characters and Conduct* contains a few critical remarks, it seems memorable now for its entertaining personal abuse. In fact, Dennis sent James Greenwood, perhaps in 1720, a copy of the Sir John letters with the simple "wish they may entertain you" (*OL*, 2:457). And the author of *The Battle of the Authors* shows appreciation for all the fun as he describes the battle of wind guns and ink squirts between Sir John's rabble and the disciplined forces of our hero, known here as "*Horatius Truewit*, who has, with a great deal of Force, Poinancy, and Vigour, attack'd the very ring-leader of Scribbling and Ignorance."[23]

Far more valuable for their critical content are *A Defence of Sir Fopling Flutter* (1722) and *Remarks on a Play, Call'd, The Conscious Lovers, a Comedy* (1723). Both were prompted by Steele's preparation for and eventual production of *The Conscious Lovers*, but the two pamphlets serve quite different purposes: *A Defence of Sir Fopling Flutter* establishes a general critical point, while the *Remarks on . . . The Conscious Lovers* delivers applied criticism of Steele's play.

The subtitle of *A Defence of Sir Fopling Flutter* clearly points up Dennis's focus upon an aesthetic question: "In which Defence is shewn, That Sir *Fopling* . . . was rightly compos'd by the Knight his Father, to answer the Ends of *Comedy;* and that he has been barbarously and scurrilously attack'd by the Knight his Brother. . . . By which it appears, That the latter Knight knows nothing of the Nature of Comedy."[24] The question arises from Steele's work on the developing genre of sentimental comedy. According to Steele, the comic protagonist must be an exemplary character. In *Spectator* 65 he assails Etherege's *The Man of Mode, or Sir Fopling Flutter* for not providing such a hero: "a fine Gentleman should be honest in his Actions, and refined in his Language. Instead of this, our Hero, in this Piece, is a direct Knave in his Designs, and a Clown in his Language."[25]

Issued five days before the premiere of *The Conscious Lovers*, Dennis's pamphlet cannot directly criticize a play not yet seen. Instead, he attacks the major critical foundation upon which he knows Steele has based his comedy. Dennis reminds us that for generations writers like Jonson, Aristotle, and Molière have rightly found comedy a way to impart moral instruction through imperfect characters: "But as Tragedy instructs chiefly by its

Design, Comedy instructs by its Characters. . . . Laughter is the Life, and the very Soul of Comedy. 'Tis its proper Business to expose Persons to our View, whose Views we may shun, and whose Follies we may despise" (*CW*, 2:245). Therefore, he concludes, Etherege does not deserve scorn for picturing corrupt human nature, since "instead of setting us Patterns for our Imitation, which is not the proper Business of *Comedy,* he makes those Follies and Vices ridiculous, which we ought to shun and despise . . . [;] the Ridicule is particularly in the Grand Incidents, and in the principal Characters. For a true Comick Poet is a Philosopher, who, like old *Democritus,* always instructs us laughing" (*CW*, 2:250).

Except for overstated cries against Steele's advance publicity for his play and against the cabal of "sordid Wretches" destroying the arts (concentrated in the preface), *A Defence of Sir Fopling Flutter* transcends its occasion to constitute a worthwhile apology for the comedy of ridicule. Its arguments could not deter audiences from making the new kind of comedy a great financial triumph; but it provides as carefully logical a Neoclassical statement of comic principle as one could wish.

Dennis felt good reason less than two months later to publish *Remarks on . . . The Conscious Lovers. A Defence of Sir Fopling Flutter* had been attacked by several pamphleteers, too many of whom somehow missed his point about the nature of true comedy. The most outrageous example is the anonymous *Sir Richard Steele, and His New Comedy, Call'd, "The Conscious Lovers," Vindicated, from the Malicious Aspersions of Mr. John Dennis* (1723). More importantly, the tremendous success of *The Conscious Lovers* marked a great turning away from his traditional idea of comedy. In addition, certain details of the play's staging and publication probably irked him. Among the male leads, for instance, were his foes Booth, Cibber, and Wilks. And in the preface Steele triumphantly addresses to "small Criticks" (Dennis in particular) a taunting song that opens, "From Place to Place forlorn I go, / With downcast Eyes a silent Shade."[26]

Remarks on . . . The Conscious Lovers consists of four sections: (1) the epistle dedicatory, (2) the preface, (3) remarks on Steele's preface to his play, and (4) remarks on *The Conscious Lovers* itself.

In the first two sections Dennis dwells mainly on his bitterness and outrage. He expresses shock that the public did not thank him for revealing Steele's theatrical fraud, which we must find exactly parallel to the South Sea Bubble fiasco: "The Generality of Mankind are sure to love him, who imposes on them, and to hate him who opens their Eyes" (*CW,* 2:253). He appeals directly to Robert Walpole for support of an art declining since the granting of a license "to four sordid Players" opened the way for stupidity and comedies scarcely "worth one Farthing" (*CW,* 2:252). However, at the end of the preface, with the help of Horace, Juvenal, and, especially, the Earl of Shaftesbury, he reasserts the integrity of critics and good writers in the face of degenerate taste and successful hacksters.

In the third section Dennis renews his attack upon Steele's theory of comedy: "When Sir *Richard* says, that any thing that has its Foundation in Happiness and Success must be the Subject of Comedy, he confounds Comedy with that Species of Tragedy which has a happy Catastrophe. When he says, that 'tis an Improvement of Comedy to introduce a Joy too exquisite for Laughter, he takes all the Care that he can to shew, that he knows nothing of the Nature of Comedy" (*CW,* 2:259). He soon makes very clear that he is reasoning on generic grounds: "that kind of Joy which is attended with Laughter, is the Characteristick of Comedy; as Terror or Compassion, according as one or the other is predominant, makes the Characteristick of Tragedy, as Admiration does of Epick Poetry" (*CW,* 2:260).

Steele, therefore, is committing a fatal artistic blunder when (in contrast to Etherege in act 2 of *The Man of Mode*) he treats the discovery in act 4 of Indiana's passion and identity in wholly nonlaughable terms. As a writer in the 28 November 1722 *Freeholder's Journal* observes, "the Discovery at last is entirely Passionate, Melting, and Tragi Comical: The Audience are sent off with a sorrowful Impression, and Tears in their Eyes, not to be wip'd off by the final Event."[27] For Dennis, such emotions have "render'd her Case deplorable, and the Catastrophe downright tragical, which of a Comedy ought to be the most comical Part, for the same Reason that it ought to be the most tragical Part of a Tragedy" (*CW,* 2:260). Unwilling to accept the possibility of Steele's developing a new type of comedy, he strictly applies a generic test to argue that his opponent has not written a comedy at all.

The final section centers on the charge that *The Conscious Lovers* is "built upon several Things which have no Foundation, either in Probability, or in Reason, or Nature" (*CW*, 2:263). Dennis finds improbable such matters as Sealand's callous disregard for his family and Bevil's concealing his passion for Indiana. Here detailed proof consists mainly in fast reminders of Aristotle, substantial quotations from Locke's *Essay on Government*, and a lengthy contrast between *The Conscious Lovers* and Terence's *Andria*, Steele's model.

The demonstration of improbabilities seems irrefutable (although Dennis does not consider how audiences might well disregard such a problem during performance—he always believes careful readers rather than theater spectators to be the only proper judges). In fact, his observation concerning improbability is picked up by other writers, most notably the author of *The Censor Censured: or, The Conscious Lovers Examin'd: in a Dialogue . . . into Which Mr. Dennis Is Introduced by Way of Postscript: with Some Conversations on His Late Remarks* (1723).

Dennis clearly enjoys an occasional verbal dart. He concludes, for instance, that Steele's diction is "affected, impure, and barbarous, and too often Hibernian" (*CW*, 2:274). The preface offers an interesting defense of such lines:

> If any one believes, that . . . I have been too harsh, and too severe, I desire such a one to consider, that I have been basely wrong'd, and barbarously us'd, by the Persons upon whom I may be thought to be too severe: And as the Wrongs which have been done me, do not come within the Cognizance of the National Law, nor under the usual Forms of the National Equity, I am as to this Matter, in a State of Nature with those Persons, and am authoriz'd by the Law of Nature to do myself Justice, as far as it may be done, without offending the Laws of my Country, or impartial Equity. (*CW*, 2:257)

Such a novel interpretation of "the Law of Nature" would let a pamphlet warrior attack almost with impunity. It certainly gives us a perspective on what critics have often viewed as the ill-tempered emotionalism of writings like *The Characters and Conduct* and the replies to Alexander Pope.

Within his pamphlets against Steele, Dennis makes a few valuable critical points. He defends criticism and artistic rules; he attacks the influence of actor-managers, the new kind of comedy, and the improbabilies of *The Conscious Lovers*. However, we too often find verbosity and desultory structure. Many pages give us repetitions of his views and deliver personal abuse. The pamphlets often entertain us, but we can ask if all the writing was worth the author's pains. Unfortunately, as Steele's protégé Benjamin Victor gloats in *An Epistle to Sir Richard Steele, on His Play, Call'd, The Conscious Lovers* (1722), Dennis only piqued the audience's curiosity about the new comedy—and helped assure still greater profits for his old friend Captain Steele.

Alexander Pope

In Alexander Pope, Dennis encountered the young adversary (only twenty-three years old at the publication of his *Essay on Criticism*) who would convince future generations that "Rinaldo Furioso" was no more than an intemperate psychopath inept at both critical and creative writing. Commentators have never agreed on how or why the quarrel started, but we can note early signs of trouble.[28]

The first years of Pope's literary career foretold his advantage in the upcoming battle with Dennis. From 1705 to 1711 he enjoyed a much more rapid progress in gaining public recognition of his talents and in making acquaintances than had the now aging critic. Much later, Gildon, following Dennis's lead, complains that when first in town Pope "had got a sort of Knack in smooth Vercification, and with it was setting up for a Wit and a Poet."[29] But Pope's earliest published works, including the *Pastorals* and *An Essay on Criticism*, demonstrate much more than smooth verse. They embody a poetic craftsmanship far superior to that found in any of Dennis's poems as well as a mental agility that would serve him well in any literary skirmish.

Furthermore, many of his letters reveal Pope to be a bright, often calculating literary strategist not so accidentally meeting helpful members of the literary establishment, covertly promoting himself, and subtly undermining others. Dennis should have seen from an episode like Pope's brilliant pummeling of Ambrose Philips in his first substantial literary quarrel that the young man could effectively demolish a reputation. Dennis in 1716 accurately describes the techniques Pope used against Philips

(*CW,* 2:104), but he seems not to have foreseen his succumbing to a like danger.

Scholars have not settled definitely upon why Pope first attacked Dennis in print. One surmise is that the two quarreled in a coffeehouse; but Dennis notes that they had met perhaps three times and makes no mention of a quarrel at such meetings. Another speculation has been that Pope was incensed at the older critic's ignoring his *Pastorals.* At least as probable is Pope's awareness that by 1711 Dennis had written his most significant criticism and was trying to maintain his reputation as a man of letters with a serious-minded fervency easily lending itself to witty ridicule. In any case, in letters to Pope, Wycherley criticizes Dennis's literary ethics, and Henry Cromwell urges Pope to outdo Dennis at tragedy as he already has at criticism, while in a 1707 rhyming letter Pope quite likely is deriding the man when he writes, "And for a Butcher's well-fed Daughter / Great *D*——*s* roar'd, like Ox at Slaughter."[30]

Thus Pope was ready by 1711 to publish remarks against Dennis in *An Essay on Criticism.* This poem contains several jibes, as in a reference to the critic's statements about dramatic rules:

> Once on a time, *La Mancha*'s Knight, they say,
> A certain *Bard* encountring on the Way,
> Discours'd in Terms as just, with Looks as Sage,
> As e'er cou'd *Dennis,* of the *Grecian* Stage;
> Concluding all were desp'rate Sots and Fools,
> Who durst depart from *Aristotle*'s Rules.

Far more personal is the infamous pair of couplets:

> 'Twere well, might Criticks still this Freedom take;
> But *Appius* reddens at each Word you speak,
> And *stares, Tremendous!* with a *threatning Eye,*
> *Like some fierce Tyrant* in *Old Tapestry!*[31]

The first passage seems little more than a standard witticism of the type that one might direct against any critic who stresses the rules with zeal. But the second, in its creative insight and poetic compression, brilliantly images a verdict of character not to be passed over. The direct reference to Dennis's recent dramatic failure, *Appius and Virginia,* clearly establishes the target in these four lines. The name "Appius" transfers to the playwright himself the ferocious distemper of his title character, while "tremendous" refers at once to the style of the play and to the author's earlier critical reflections upon greatness and high emotion in poetry. Thus Dennis the person, the dramatist, and the critic takes on an immoderate violence of character that before Pope no commentators had observed. Furthermore, the thumping alliteration of the two final lines (similar to that found in Old English verse) with the image of permanently woven "Old Tapestry" poetically states that this character sketch is in truth an old, unalterable story.

Dennis felt the power in Pope's lines, but he lacked the good sense to let the matter drop or the gift of cutting poetic riposte that might have countered the character sketch more effectively. Instead, in the next month he rushed into print *Reflections Critical and Satyrical, upon a Late Rhapsody, Call'd, An Essay upon Criticism.* Although not effectively organized, probably because of Dennis's usual haste, there is a rough structure, as he first vents his indignation, then proceeds through five reasons that the author of the *Essay on Criticism* must be a youth, and ends with a flurry of charges amid much vituperation.

In the preface we learn why Dennis has felt compelled to write the *Reflections Critical and Satyrical.* "Attack'd without any manner of Provocation on my side, and attack'd in my Person, instead of my Writings" in a poem bristling with indifferent thoughts, execrable verse, and shallow judgment, he must respond (*CW,* 1:396). The popularity of the "little affected Hyprocrite" who penned *An Essay on Criticism* only further illustrates the national depravity of genius and taste. Pope is never referred to by name, since he published his poem anonymously; in Dennis's mind Pope's not signing his name heightens the immorality of the attack. The preface ends with a breathless roar against undeservedly popular authors who, like rogues, libel and lampoon others.

Through most of the *Reflections Critical and Satyrical* proper, a letter addressed to a fictional "Mr. ———— at Sunning-Hill, Berks.," Dennis proposes five reasons that his assailant must be "some young, or some raw Author" (*CW,* 1:397–98). The

underlying source of disgruntlement here, not directly acknowledged, is that a long-established writer who has defended literature and constructed his theories with the utmost care and
patience could be rudely put in his place by a few lines penned
by an insolent young upstart.

He notes first that Pope "hath rashly undertaken a Task which
is infinitely above his Force." Next, "While this little Author
struts and affects the Dictatorian Air, he plainly shews that at
the same time he is under the Rod; and that while he pretends
to give Laws to others, he is himself a pedantick Slave to Authority and Opinion" (*CW,* 1:398). Proofs lie in Pope's wrong-
headed insinuation that only great poets can be good critics
and his "servile Deference" to the ancients. Third, Pope has
cheapened the material borrowed from the Earls of Mulgrave
and Roscommon. Fourth, the poet frequently contradicts himself. Finally, Pope is always wrong. This last point receives elabo-
ration in several pages of oftentimes quite accurate yet tedious
examinations of one line of verse after another.

Dennis concludes his main section with a summary of Pope's
youthful liabilities:

Thus are his Assertions, and his Precepts frequently false or trivial,
or both, his Thoughts very often crude and abortive, his Expressions
absurd, his Numbers often harsh and unmusical, without Cadence
and without Variety, his Rhimes trivial and common. He dictates perpetually, and pretends to give Law without any thing of the Simplicity
or Majesty of a Legislator, and pronounces Sentence without any thing
of the Plainness or Clearness, or Gravity of a Judge. Instead of Simplicity we have little Conceit and Epigram, and Affectation. Instead of
Majesty we have something that is very mean, and instead of Gravity
we have something that is very boyish. And instead of Perspicuity
and lucid Order, we have but too often Obscurity and Confusion.
(*CW,* 1:413–14)

Such concentrated censure leads naturally into a fast complaint
against the poet's insolence and then the final section.

The concluding charges make interesting reading but receive
woefully inadequate support. For one thing, Pope is accused
of Jacobitism. Dennis weakly reasons that Pope's criticism of
kings makes him a Jacobite; actually, probably more important
factors contributing to this judgment are Dennis's knowledge

of Pope's Catholicism and his own extreme fear of Jacobitism, such as we find in several letters written at this time. Also weakly made are charges that Pope has violated all ethics by stealthily eroding Dryden's reputation and by signing Wycherley's name to verses Pope had written in his own praise.

Before the third section, personal rancor has run through most paragraphs, as seen, for instance, in the continuous reference to Pope's "little" stature as objective fact and as metaphor for his mental and moral unworthiness. But at the end vituperation completely dominates. Dennis relishes putting the "young, squab, short Gentleman" in his rightful place: "Instead of setting his Picture to show, I have taken a keener Revenge, and expos'd his Intellectuals, as duly considering that let the Person of a Gentleman of his Parts be never so contemptible, his inward Man is ten times more ridiculous; it being impossible that his outward Form, tho' it should be that of a downright Monkey, should differ so much from human Shape, as his immaterial unthinking part does from human Understanding" (*CW,* 1:417).

Critics from the eighteenth to the twentieth century have labeled the *Reflections Critical and Satyrical* "frantic and illiberal" and "very angry and ill-natured."[32] Unfortunately, Dennis utterly failed to foresee Pope's far more complex response. The young poet did not simply retort with one more pamphlet of straightforward abuse. In the first place, he made for later editions of *An Essay on Criticism* several revisions as suggested by Dennis. Such action might indicate to contemporary readers that Pope could assess the pamphlet with rationality and the willingness to learn, in contrast to his opponent's irascibility.

But Pope had still more delectable plans for revenge, as he first suggests in letters written within five days of the publication of *Reflections Critical and Satyrical* (which the publisher, Lintot, had shown him before publication). He clearly finds Dennis to have set himself up as an easy target. The critic has gone to excessive lengths to ridicule physical traits, quibble over numerous individual lines (*Reflections Critical and Satyrical* even contains appended "Annotations," or further quibbles), and explode in almost incoherent fury. Pamphlet revenge indeed crashes upon Dennis with *The Critical Specimen* (1711) and *The Narrative of Dr. Robert Norris* (1713), both convincingly attributed to Pope by Norman Ault.[33]

Using an imaginative approach foreign to his adversary, Pope offers in *The Critical Specimen* a mock-advertisement for a nonexistent "Treatise in *Folio*" entitled *The Mirror of Criticisme: or, The History of the Renown'd Rinaldo Furioso, Critick of the Woful Countenance.* Extravagances and whimsies are manufactured or ludicrously magnified in a spirit of malevolent fun.

A sample chapter shows how Dennis's self-delusion appears worse than Don Quixote's as his "Head *Sublime*" gasps Parnassian air and gulps Aganippe's waters. In the full list of chapter titles, Pope jabs at both writings and character. Ridiculing the unpopular comedy *Gibraltar,* for instance, he promises to write "of the Bombarding of *Gibraltar,* and how several of the Cheifs engaged in this dreadful enterprise were contrary to the Law of Arms, almost pelted to Death with *Apples* and *Orange-Peel.*" He derides a perhaps fabricated wish on Dennis's part to make greater thunder for a play like *Appius and Virginia* with "his Invention of a wonderful *Mustard Bowl* of a prodigious Size for the Players to make *Thunder* with."

We hear also of his aversion for catcalls, his fussiness over his shoes and breeches, and his morbid fear that the King of France wishes to throw him into prison. And Pope exults in his own technical cleverness in using phrases from *Reflections Critical and Satyrical* against Dennis, as when the old critic becomes a venomous amphibian: "A baneful *Hunch-back'd Toad,* with look Maligne, / Glares on some Traveller's unwary steps."[34]

Even greater satiric damage is wreaked in *The Narrative of Dr. Robert Norris, Concerning the Strange and Deplorable Frenzy of Mr. John Denn—— An Officer of the Custom-House,* published shortly after *Remarks upon Cato.* Pope achieves a measure of credibility by using the name of an actual Robert Norris, who advertised himself "Robert Norris at the Pestle and Mortar on Snow Hill . . . many years experienc'd in the Care of Lunaticks."[35]

The persona takes us into the critic's chambers, in which manuscripts litter the floor and a confused old woman attempts to guard her begrimed master, recently bewitched by a mysterious *"Cator."* Poor old Dennis sees newcomers as King Louis's agents and roars at pages of *Cato* pinned to the wall. His mental distress leads him to rave, "Is all the Town in a Combination? Shall

Poetry fall to the ground? Must our Reputation be lost to all foreign Countries? O Destruction! Perdition! *Opera! Opera!* As Poetry once rais'd a City, so when Poetry fails, Cities are over-turn'd, and the World is no more." After an ill-fated attempt to bind him, his attendants incur a barrage of bandages, glasses, blood, folios, and a peruke block—Dennis obviously proves himself a lunatic.

This point being established, Pope then sneaks in a few anec-dotes for which he has prepared us. For example, upon reading two lines about critics in general in *An Essay on Criticism,* "He flung down the Book in a terrible Fury, and cried out, *By G—— he means Me.*"[36] Pope has skillfully woven half-truths and untruths into a fast-paced character sketch so well done that we almost have to believe it—and many later critics have.

Although he did not respond immediately, Dennis keenly felt the power of the ridicule. The sting carries into his *A True Character of Mr. Pope, and His Writings* (1716), published anony-mously as part of Edmund Curll's revenge against the poet.[37] Ostensibly provoked by an unidentified libel (about the exact nature of which Dennis is uncharacteristically vague) and written in considerable structural disarray, the brief attack breathlessly delivers a flurry of charges, including the unsupported claim that Pope had teased Bernard Lintot into publishing Dennis's *Remarks upon Cato.* It opens with a character of Pope written by another hand (probably Charles Gildon's), which hits hard at this "Rhimester without Judgment or Reason, and a Critick without Common Sense; a Jesuitical Professor of Truth, a base and a foul Pretender to Candour; a Barbarous Wretch, who is perpetually boasting of Humanity and Good Nature, a lurking way-laying Coward, and a Stabber in the Dark; who is always pretending to Magnanimity, and to sum up all Villains in one, a Traytor-Friend, one who has betrayed all Mankind . . ." (*CW,* 2:103). In Dennis's own pages charges tumble one upon an-other, but we can discern his focus upon two, Pope's libelous criticism of other writers and his execrable imitations of ge-niuses, most notably Horace and Homer.

Dennis's anger boils over with its greatest vitriolism when he lambasts his opponent's criticism. For example, he typically finds Pope the libeler "the most Impudent, and the most Incorri-gible, who has lately pester'd and plagu'd the World with Five

or Six Scandalous Libels, in Prose, that are all of them at once
so Stupid, and so Malicious, that Men of Sense are Doubtful,
if they should attribute them to the Libellers Native Idiotism,
or to Accidental Madness" (*CW*, 2:107). He seems here to
be reproducing the malignity of an offensive like *The Narrative
of Dr. Robert Norris*, but we totally miss the creativity that can
render malignity enjoyable.

The meanest lines that Dennis ever wrote occur in this pamphlet as he castigates Pope for his physical deformities. On the
title page he quotes from the Earl of Rochester abusive lines
such as "A Lump Deform'd and Shapeless was he Born." Deriding the "Ludicrous Animal's" hunched back, he hurls malicious
name-calling at one "who, as he is in Shape a *Monkey*, is so in
his every Action; in his senseless Chattering, and his merry Gri-
maces, in his doing hourly Mischief and hiding himself, in the
variety of his Ridiculous Postures, and his continual Shiftings,
from Place to Place, from Persons to Persons, from Thing to
Thing" (*CW*, 2:104).

We sense at times an even more discomfiting note. This we
feel especially when Dennis upbraids Pope for

his Natural Deformity, which did not come by his own Fault, but
seems to be the Curse of God upon him; we desire that Person to
consider, that this little Monster has upbraided People with their Calamities and their Diseases, and Calamities and Diseases, which are
either false or past, or which he himself gave them by administring
Poison to them; we desire that Person to consider, that Calamities
and Diseases, if they are neither false nor past, are common to all
Men; that a Man can no more help his Calamities and his Diseases,
than a Monster can his Deformity; that there is no Misfortune, but
what the Generality of Mankind are liable too, and that there is no
one Disease, but what all the rest of Men are subject too; whereas
the Deformity of this Libeller, is Visible, Present, Lasting, Unalterable,
and Peculiar to himself. 'Tis the mark of God and Nature upon him,
to give us warning that we should hold no Society with him, as a
Creature not of our Original, nor of our Species. (*CW*, 2:105)

In these lines our critic writhes with a hatred of great intensity.
In fact, *A True Character of Mr. Pope* was powerful enough to
inspire an anonymous 1740 poem, *The Blatant Beast*, which
likewise sees in Pope's physiognomy signs of his inner deformity:

> Distorted Elf! to Nature a Disgrace,
> Thy Mind envenom'd pictur'd in thy Face;
> Malice with Envy in thy Breast combines,
> And in thy Visage grav'd those ghastly Lines.[38]

Unfortunately, the very depth of hatred in *A True Character of Mr. Pope* also throws its author out of control. He loses his usual judiciousness and convincing mastery of verifiable detail.

Pope again appeared the more rational disputant by refusing to engage in such open viciousness. Instead, he joined Gay and Arbuthnot in composing *Three Hours after Marriage* (1717), a rollicking farce containing rather temperate jibes at Dennis's intemperance. Actually, after the publication of *The Narrative of Dr. Robert Norris,* Pope was too busily engaged in other projects to worry much about Dennis, who was but one of many writers attacking the poet. Dennis's career seemed almost at a standstill in contrast to Pope's success with *The Rape of the Lock* (1714), *The Temple of Fame* (1715), and *The Iliad of Homer* (1715–20).

The enthusiastic reception of the *Iliad* translation prompted Dennis to publish his next anti-Pope work. Especially galling was the 5 January 1717 issue of the *Censor,* in which Lewis Theobald highly praises the new Homer translation. Theobald manages also to ridicule Dennis, "the modern *Furius,*" because "a Critic of this Complexion sets up in defiance of good Sense, and is a professed Foe to every Excellency which he cannot reach: He is the Reverse of a *Knight-Errant,* prowling about to *destroy,* as the Other to *defend.* . . . more the Object of *Pity,* than that which he daily provokes, Laughter and Contempt."

Dennis's *Remarks upon Mr. Pope's Translation of Homer. With Two Letters Concerning Windsor Forest, and The Temple of Fame* (1717) gathers several pieces of criticism. Although unified on the topic of Pope, they are a disparate mixture composed of a preface assailing Pope's undeserved popularity, observations upon the translation (with some ridicule of Theobald), a 1714 letter to Barton Booth on *Windsor Forest,* a 1715 letter on *The Temple of Fame,* and a postscript including a disagreement with Mme Dacier and a discussion of the word *murmur.*

Critics have mostly agreed that the pamphlet contributes little to its author's reputation. Indeed, two major weaknesses seem painfully obvious: the transparent bias and the refusal to judge *Windsor Forest* and *The Temple of Fame* on their own merits. But the critics at the same time overlook the strengths that make *Remarks upon Mr. Pope's Translation of Homer* far more worthwhile than *A True Character of Mr. Pope.*

We cannot overlook the strong bias against Pope's physique, religion, and success. Dennis again scatters automatic references to "this Little *Ass,*" "the little Gentleman," or "this little Author." Stronger in this pamphlet are the strikes against the poet's Roman Catholicism. He is accused of attempting "to suborn Old HOMER to propagate his ridiculous Arbitrary and Popish Doctrines" (*CW,* 2:119). The only proofs of such an assertion consist in a brief analysis of the Jacobite implications of one couplet and a tangential cry against Pope's *A Roman Catholick Version of the First Psalm* (1716), authored by "a Popish Rhymester [who] has been brought up with a Contempt for those Sacred Writings in the Language which he understands. So that Ignorance with such a one, is the true Mother of Devotion" (*CW,* 2:130). As spirited as they may be, the slashes at Pope's deformity and religion never touch directly on the quality of the translation.

Dennis is again perturbed mostly at the success of this poet, who "tho' an Empty, has been a Popular Scribbler" (*CW,* 2:119). Citing the opinions of Horace, Juvenal, Dryden, and Jonson, Dennis concludes that the "vilest Scribblers" have always been popular. One consequence has been the undeserved hardships incurred by such able writers as Ambrose Philips, Butler, Dryden, and Congreve. Pope's unmerited success, nurtured by a time of "Epidemical Stupidity" that has also nurtured fanatics like Henry Sacheverell, portends the second, more dangerous potential consequence of religious and political ruin. Thus, when the "notorious Ideot" Theobald promotes the new *Iliad,* he is committing more than a silly error.

As clearly as Dennis places the translator's popularity within a broader context, we feel lurking the envy of a now scorned author—although he explicitly gets no closer to his own predicament than to say, "I am very unwilling to acquaint the Reader with what has happen'd in my own Memory" (*CW,* 2:118). The heavy emphasis upon empty reputation, however, lends the pamphlet an unpleasant overtone.

In "Observations upon *Windsor Forest,*" Dennis actually has little to say of the poem. It is, in general, "a wretched Rhapsody, not worthy the Observation of a Man of Sense" written in lines "Obscure, Ambiguous, Affected, Temerarious, Barbarous" (*CW,* 2:135, 137). The only particular observation notes that the poem describes trifling objects not peculiar to this one forest. However, Dennis contrasts Pope's rural poem with John Denham's *Cooper's Hill* (1642), on which he lavishes enthusiastically detailed praise for its "admirable Art and Contrivance." Denham receives loving attention; Pope receives contempt through lack of attention. Perhaps Dennis errs in placing the letter to Barton Booth in this 1717 critique focusing on Pope, because when he wrote the letter in 1714, he was trying quite simply "to display the Beauties of *Cooper's-Hill*" (*CW,* 2:135).

Dennis makes perhaps the most amazing blunder of his career in the letter on *The Temple of Fame.* He somehow disregards Pope's opening advertisement and many notes directly identifying the poem as an imitation of Chaucer's *House of Fame.* Overlooking, moreover, the poem's dramatic structure, imaginative power, and passages of notable inventiveness (such as the young Pope's finally viewing himself as a rash "Candidate for Praise"), Dennis objects to what he finds to be lines of obfuscation and illogic.

Unfortunately, a great deal of the objectionable material comes straight from Chaucer. Thus Dennis derides as inexcusable the descriptive images that readers have long found appealing in the old dream vision. He does rightly note some lines needing revision, but his own effort seems lost in his inattentiveness to the purpose and tone of *The Temple of Fame.* An odd paragraph in a 1728 letter indicates his belated recognition of Pope's source: "Tho' I have not for several Years read *Chaucer's Temple of Fame,* yet I am well enough acquainted with his Character, to know that he has too much Genius, and too much good Sense to have committed many Absurdities; whereas the *Temple of Fame,* writ by the *Pantomimical A. P——E,* is one long Chain of Blunders and Boggisms, and one continued Absurdity" (*CW,* 2:417). Dennis realizes that he has erred, but he obscures his fault with one more *ad hominem* argument.

The pages on the *Iliad,* happily, contain much of merit. Dennis knows the original well. He admires Homer's figurative language, purity, brightness, and grace. He knows also the difficulties faced by Pope or any other Homeric translator:

Indeed it is impossible for any Translator, and much less for this, to express in a Translation the Poetical Language of HOMER. By the Advantage of the Language in which he wrote, he had several ways of rendering his Language Poetical, which a Translator can never have; as the frequent Use of compounded and decompounded Words; the Use of Words which were as it were at one and the same time both Grecian and Foreign; as being confin'd in their vulgar Use to some particular Part of *Greece;* as likewise the Use of Words which were purely Poetick, and which were seldom or never us'd in Prose; the contracting or lengthening the Words which he used, and the frequent transposing of Syllables; and, lastly, the altering the Terminations of Words, by means of the different Dialects. (*CW,* 2:123)

Dennis clearly is going into his criticism with expertise and a fairminded notion of what Pope faces.

As we read his reactions to Pope's lines (he focuses on the first one hundred lines of the new *Iliad*), one particular strength emerges: the very closeness of the reading. Dennis demonstrates a keen eye for obscurities, changes of tone or character, unsure rhythm, indecorum, and nonidiomatic diction. We can quickly see much of his procedure in his treatment of one couplet:

Ver. 27.

> *But O! releive a wretched Parent's Pain,*
> *And give* CHRYSEIS *to these Arms again.*

This is the Language of a Lover, and by its Levity and Affectation, corrupts the Simplicity and Gravity of the Original, and destroys the Character of CHRYSES; of whom it is very unbecoming, either as a Man in Years, a Father, or a Priest. HOMER says only,

> *Set free my dear Daughter.* (*CW,* 2:129)

We cannot say that Dennis is always careful or fair—he misquotes lines and refuses to find any worth at all in the translation—but he is thorough. At times his penetrating verbal analysis of a line reminds us of his line-by-line rigorousness in *The Impar-*

tial Critick. He says, in effect, that as totally as he may ridicule this *Iliad,* it is in fact a book that must be read closely if we are to judge it properly; he implies that he is a critic able to perform such a necessary task. We find in a 20 September 1716 letter evidence of his difficulty in achieving such a tone as he laments that he is trying to discuss the new Homer translation without prejudice, but "to make Remarks upon this—(Death and Hell!) a Man must read it" (*OL,* 1:127).

At the same time, these observations on the *Iliad* can entertain us. Dennis can rip into Pope's lines with sprightliness, as when he complains of two lines, "By the English Translation one would think, that AGAMEMNON had sent the old Priest a Challenge. O wicked, wicked Rhyme! what Errors, what Blunders art not thou the Occasion of, in lazy and ignorant Poetasters!" (*CW,* 2:129).

He cannot discern any marvelous ability transferring from Homer to the English translator: "one would swear, that he had a Hill in *Tipperary,* for his *Parnassus,* and a Puddle in some Bog, for his *Hippocrene.*" Or in a like vein, "The *Pegasus* of this little Gentleman, is not the Steed that HOMER rode; but a blind, stumbling *Kentish* Post-Horse, which neither walks, nor trots, nor paces, nor runs; but is upon an eternal *Canterbury,* and often stumbles, and often falls. The *Pegasus* which HOMER rode, would carry Fifty POPES upon his Back at a time, and throw every one of his Riders" (*CW,* 2:124, 135). In contrast to his first two pamphlets against the little gentleman, *Remarks upon Mr. Pope's Translation of Homer,* on the whole, attacks Pope with more wittiness than meanness, with more coolness than panicked anger.

Between 1717 and 1728 hostilities between the two men pretty much ceased, Pope going so far as to subscribe to his adversary's *Select Works.* However, the poet's restlessly creative mind retained details to be used in future attacks. Thus, when in 1728 Pope found himself ready to attack literary pretentiousness, he ridiculed Dennis in two publications that provoked Dennis's last two critical pamphlets.

The first of these works by Pope, *Peri Bathous: or, Martinus Scriblerus His Treatise of the Art of Sinking in Poetry,* inverts Longinus's (and, of course, Dennis's) thoughts about literary excellence. Martinus argues that since our most common end in literature is mediocrity, we should codify rules that let us easily achieve literary depths. Serving as a convenient example, Dennis is ridiculed as literary stylist and critic.

In the role of one of the "Genius's in the *Profund,*" he is metaphorically grouped with porpoises, which "are unwieldly and big; they put all their Numbers into a great *Turmoil* and *Tempest,* but whenever they appear in *plain Light* (which is seldom) they are only *shapeless* and *ugly Monsters.*" A mangled quotation from Dennis's "A Pindarick Ode on the King . . . Occasion'd by the Victory at *Aghrim*" illustrates anticlimax, one of the *"Diminishing* Figures." Finally, Pope ascribes to Dennis and Gildon a nonexistent pamphlet, *A Project for the Advancement of the Stage,* which promotes bathos through such means as naming "the *oldest Poet* and *Critick* to be found in the whole Island" (namely, Dennis) the president of all writers.[39]

Also published in this year was the first edition of *The Dunciad.* Here Dennis is again attacked, but with nothing like the severity of the next year's edition. He incurs scattered jibes—for example, he can make thunder in a mustard bowl, and he wins admiration in a diving contest as he sinks deeply. But Pope does not single out the aging critic for any kind of sustained censure.

Dennis, however, found it incredible that Pope should attack him at all. He thus published in 1728 *Remarks on Mr. Pope's Rape of the Lock. In Several Letters to a Friend. With a Preface, Occasion'd by the Late Treatise on the Profund, and The Dunciad.* The preface, obviously, was written shortly before publication. The seven letters, originally written in 1714, were probably revised in or after 1717.[40]

Dennis claims in his preface that he finished the letters years earlier but "took care to keep back the ensuing Treatise purposely *in Terrorem;* which had so good an Effect, that he [Pope] endeavour'd for some time to counterfeit Humility and a sincere Repentance" (*CW,* 2:322). With breathless anger like that found in *Reflections Critical and Satyrical,* he rushes on to accuse "Mr. *A. P——E*" of proving himself a "Fool, Dunce, Blockhead, Scoundrel" by calling others those names. This author of "the insipid *Profund*" and "the fulsome *Dunciad*" has basely convinced a degenerate world that a writer's poverty signifies his lack of artistic merit.

Letter I focuses mainly on Pope's title page "creating in his

Readers an Expectation of Pleasantry, when there is not so much as one Jest in his Book" (*CW*, 2:328). In letter II Dennis contends that because *The Rape of the Lock,* in contrast to Boileau's *Le Lutrin,* is a trifle, it can have neither fable nor moral nor mirth-provoking incidents. According to letter III Pope's Belinda is not a character, since her beauty depends on artifice and she is represented inconsistently, seeming first a fine lady and afterwards "an arrant Tramp and a Tomrigg" (*CW*, 2:334).

Dennis establishes in letter IV a complex critical argument proving his opponent's machines (spirits) unsatisfactory. He concludes that "his Machines contradict the Doctrines of the Christian Religion, contradict all sound Morality; there is no allegorical nor sensible Meaning in them; and for these Reasons they give no Instruction, make no Impression at all upon the Mind of a sensible Reader. Instead of making the Action wonderful and delightful, they render it extravagant, absurd, and incredible. They do not in the least influence that Action . . ." (*CW*, 2:337).

Letters V and VI introduce numerous illustrations of the poet's trivial and extravagant sentiments. Dennis particularly loathes "the *Puns* which are every where spread throughout it. *Puns* bear the same Proportion to *Thought,* that *Bubbles* hold to *Bodies,* and may justly be compared to those gaudy Bladders which Children make with Soap; which, tho' they please their weak Capacities with a momentary Glittering, yet are but just beheld, and vanish into Air" (*CW*, 2:347). The final letter attacks Pope's syntax in the first twelve lines of the poem.

Remarks on Mr. Pope's Rape of the Lock failed to counter Pope's growing advantage in the controversy. The preface once again shows Dennis acting the role of furious hypercritic. Meanwhile, except for some of the more thoughtful material in letter IV, the criticism within the letters seems totally beside the point. Essentially, Dennis fails to judge *The Rape of the Lock* by standards of mock-heroic poetry, insisting that all in the poem must be grandly heroic, unmixed, and serious. He at times goes through the motions of careful investigation but almost seems to be trying to misjudge the poem. Indeed, Hooker, usually a staunch defender of Dennis, admits that the pamphlet "is fundamentally wrong and fundamentally bad. Its fundamental wrongness, however, is not the result of mere anger or perversity. Dennis had no sympathy with the 'fairy way of writing.' By nature and temperament he was committed to high seriousness and to a belief that literature should deal realistically with the important concerns of civilized men. Consequently he was unable to understand or enjoy the exquisite trifling of the *Rape*" (*CW,* 2:513–14).

In 1729 Pope issued *The Dunciad Variorum.* James Sutherland carefully describes in the introduction and notes to the Twickenham edition of *The Dunciad* how Pope first provoked authors to write against him and then incorporated their remarks. His campaign worked best against Dennis. Indeed, the 1729 edition constitutes the coup de grace against Dennis's reputation.

The Dunciad Variorum employs an amazing variety of techniques to convince us that Dennis must surely be counted a premier dunce of the literary world. As early as the frontispiece, Pope is ridiculing his opponent with fine subtlety. The 1728 version pictures the owl of antiquity atop a pile of books including *Dennis's Works,* a slight volume for so "tremendous" and prolific an author. With the 1729 version this slender work remains (all others but Theobald's having been replaced), now on a load of books across an ass's back. At the opposite end of the book, the index lists under Dennis's name such topics as "Esteem'd by our Author and why," "His love of Puns," and "His Excuse for Obscenity in Plays"—all anathema to the old man.[41]

Between these two sections Pope works brilliantly in both verse and prose. The verse satire consists usually of brief yet effective references, as in

> The Monkey-mimicks rush discordant in.
> 'Twas chatt'ring, grinning, mouthing, jabb'ring all,
> And Noise, and Norton Brangling, and Breval,
> Dennis and Breval,
> Dennis and Dissonance. . . .[42]

Here the final alliteration within the context of dissonance clearly affirms that all of Dennis's words at last come down to the mere noise characteristic of the dunces' nonsense.

Even more effective are the mock notes. For example, the single line "And all the Mighty Mad in Dennis rage" occasions two lengthy footnotes heavy with irony, other writers' opinions of Dennis, and quotations from him at his meanest or most inane, all establishing as verified fact the old man's mental instability. Many quotations from Dennis—now put into a strange new context—are attacks upon Pope. The poet interprets such quotations: "The reader, who has seen thro' the course of these notes, what a constant attendance Mr *D.* paid to our Author and all his works, may perhaps wonder he should be mention'd but twice, and so slightly touch'd, in this poem. But in truth he look'd upon him with some esteem, for having (more generously than all the rest) *set his Name* to such writings."[43]

Much the same strategy underlies such "scholarly" apparatus as "Testimonies of Authors Concerning our Poet and his Works" and "A List of Books, Papers, and Verses, in which our Author was abused," all saturated with Dennis's more hostile remarks. Pope, with all his seeming fairness and meticulousness, creatively persuades us that Dennis has proven himself a mad dunce.

Innumerable explosions of pained anger were hurled by the dunces and their supporters against Pope, "a *Scoundrel, or Blockhead,* who has, at one Time or other, *Betrayed* or *Abused* almost every one he has conversed with."[44] One of the saner, more valuable responses is Dennis's last critical pamphlet, *Remarks upon Several Passages in the Preliminaries to the Dunciad. . . . And upon Several Passages in Pope's Preface to His Translation of Homer's Iliad* (1729).

While this pamphlet often labels Pope impudent, foolish, and ignorant, it does not convey the senseless frenzy of a desperate man that so often mars Dennis's earlier responses to his opponent. He now seems, in fact, wholly aware that a tone of noncontrol would only weaken his case. Thus he explains how he has just reread his earlier writings on Pope, "and some of them after a very long Distance of Time from the first writing and publishing them; so that the warm and partial Conceit of an Author had been a long time extinguish'd" (*CW,* 2:355). In the present remarks he is attempting to achieve the tone of impartiality that informs his earliest criticism and only seems to inform the notes and appendixes of *The Dunciad Variorum.*

In its content the pamphlet delivers more substance than Dennis's other anti-Pope writings. His observations show considera-

ble variety: Pope has deposed Lewis Theobald as King of
Dunces; throughout his relationship with Dennis, Pope has been
guilty of lies and "monstrous Perfidy" (as in maneuvering Bernard Lintot into printing *Remarks upon Cato*); Pope wrongly
views Homer as an unsophisticated genius; he underrates "the
Transcendency of *Milton*'s Genius"; the "Letter to the Publisher" (in *The Dunciad Variorum*) must have been written by
Pope; he has grossly misrepresented Giles Jacob's use of materi-
als submitted by Pope and Dennis; Boileau is superior to Pope.
Of primary importance is the still valuable argument that Pope

sings Books, and not an Action; and the Author who pretends in an
Epick Poem to sing Books instead of singing an Action, is only qualified
to sing Ballads. . . .
    P. is so far from singing an Action, that there is no such Thing as
Action in his whimsical Rhapsody. . . . The Thing is divided into
Three Books. In the First, instead of Action there is Description and
Declamation. In the Third, instead of Action we have nothing but a
feverish Dream. The Second is made up of Nastiness, Obscenity, and
Absurdity; and is so far from being Part of an Action, that it runs
counter to the Design of the whole Thing, if there could be any
Design in it; for Vigour of Action can never proceed from Dulness,
though it may from Madness. The Hero of the Piece does nothing
at all, and never speaks but once, unless it be half a Line in the Third
Book. (*CW,* 2:361)

Dennis also varies his techniques. He appeals to our sense
of fair play; develops close logical sequences; applies treatises
by Dacier and Le Bossu; reprints letters from Jacob, Pope,
Steele, Gildon, and himself. He has worked diligently and for
the most part coolly.

With this pamphlet Dennis wrote his most effective response
to Pope. Unfortunately, it was not enough to counter the accepted interpretation of Dennis the old Furius firmly imprinted
on the public consciousness by Pope's artistry. After 1729 the
two men ceased their full-scale warfare, Dennis recognizing that
he had done all in his power, Pope seeing no gain from devising
new attacks against the aging writer.

By the end of Dennis's career, in fact, Pope was perhaps
indirectly sending him financial aid. For the 1733 benefit performance of *The Provok'd Husband,* Pope anonymously supplied

the "Prologue, For the Benefit of Mr. Dennis." Calling attention to the "Spectacle of Woe! / Wept by each Friend, forgiv'n by ev'ry Foe," he celebrates

> *Dennis,* who long had warr'd with modern *Huns,*
> Their Quibbles routed, and defy'd their Puns;
> A desp'rate Bulwark, sturdy, firm, and fierce,
> Against the *Gothick* Sons of frozen Verse;
> How chang'd from him, who made the Boxes groan,
> And shook the Stage with Thunders all his own!
> Stood up to dash each vain Pretender's Hope,
> Maul the *French* Tyrant, or pull down the Pope![45]

The poet indeed resurrects some of his old jokes against Dennis, but he also works in considerable praise. The prologue reads like the only truly balanced account Pope ever wrote of Dennis.

Chapter Four

Plays

A Plot, and No Plot

A Plot, and No Plot, first performed at Drury Lane in April or May 1697, marks Dennis's debut as a playwright. *Jacobite Credulity,* the subtitle added to the text printed in *The Select Works,* promises that the play will attack the Jacobites, those supporters of the Stuart cause, some of whom the year before had conspired in the infamous Assassination Plot. This scheme Dennis labels "the late damnable Design" in his *Remarks on . . . Prince Arthur* (*CW,* 1:54). But, as much as the first-night audience may have looked forward to and applauded his satiric political strokes, anti-Jacobitism constitutes only a minor element in the drama.

Bull Senior, a wealthy old banker with Jacobite leanings, demands that his ward Sylvia wed his cloddish son Bull Junior. However, with the assistance of the player Baldernoe, the infamous bawd Frowzy, and her daughter Friskit, Bull Senior's bright and honest nephew Belvil takes advantage of Bull Senior's political credulity to win Sylvia for himself.

Act 1 bubbles with spirit as Baldernoe wittily boasts of his disguises and Belvil curses a "Northern Monster" whom Bull Senior would have him marry. Less interesting are the lengthy expository passages in which the young men outline their plot to gull Bull Senior into joining a nonexistent Jacobite conspiracy, the consequences of which he can escape only by letting Belvil marry Sylvia. At the same time, Frowzy will convince the old man that she is a French countess whose daughter Bull Junior should marry. Bull Senior shows the requisite gullibility as he blindly characterizes himself as a great statesman "forc'd to stand buff against all the various Whiffs that come puffing" and loudly boasts that he is not a wit (*SW,* 2:298, 303).

The intrigue begins to work in earnest with the vibrant Frowzy's entrance. Surveying the playhouse audience, she provides lusty comedy as she complains about her "Phiz" ("face") and jests about her "vertuous" sexual prowess. Sylvia sees that she cannot wed Bull Junior upon hearing him yearn to visit a whore the day before his wedding and deliver obtuse lines like "I hope my Judgment may be taken for a foolish thing as soon as another Man's" (*SW*, 2:315). Unfortunately, Dennis writes very dull lines as Friskit parleys with a young man and Belvil holds a comedy-of-manners lovers' debate with Sylvia.

Bull Junior is duped into marrying Friskit after she feigns hysteria when told of his engagement to another. Assuming the title Viscount Dorant, he courts this "noble" lady by proving his own nobility. Of course, he demonstrates only obtuseness as he proclaims, "Rot me, I am a Dunce" and offers a silly love song asking, "My trembling Heart goes pit-a-pat, / Can you not guess what I'd be at?" (*SW*, 2:329, 330).

Bull Senior becomes fully ensnared when he greedily agrees to marry his son into the countess's rich family. Fast-change disguises sweep him into believing Baldernoe the French marquis prepared to lead the revolution, to whom he pledges a thousand pounds. Baldernoe reenters as a constable to arrest the old man. The fast bustle, Bull Senior's confused bluster, many asides, and a fine drinking song by Wycherley make this action highly entertaining.

A prisoner within his own home, which he believes to be Newgate Prison, Bull Senior saves himself by agreeing to let Belvil marry Sylvia. Several pages of slapstick humor deriving from his confusion lead to his recognition of his own gullibility. Belvil delivers the moral: one must not pursue bare titles, and "Credulity in Men engag'd in a Party, proceeds oftner from Pride than Weakness" (*SW*, 2:370).

Like most of Dennis's other dramatic work, *A Plot, and No Plot* did not prompt any great deal of excitement. Dennis notes in his preface the audience's good humor, and the play ran several nights. Contemporary authors usually point out the regularity with which he observes the unities (as he also does in the "Advertisement"), but that could not be sufficient to make this play entertaining. Rather, as Dennis again notes, "regularity in a Comedy, signifies little without Diversion" (*CW*, 1:145). The regularity lies particularly in focusing all the action upon the duping of the old man. But the really enjoyable elements for the audience must have been such "Diversion" as Bull Senior's confused explosions, Frowzy's indelicate patter, and the surely clownish delivery of prologue and epilogue by Joe Haines, who pleads, "Now, tho this Play perhaps may show no brains, / Yet spare this Prologue, which was writ by *Hains.*"[1] In other words, as much as Dennis the theorist may hope that his play reflects advancement in comedy, the success it enjoyed probably derives from its farcical elements.

The 1734 *Life* observes, "This Comedy is so diverting, that it is very surprizing that none of the wise Managers of the Stage have ever thought it worth reviveing. . . ."[2] The play did indeed enjoy an April 1746 revival (following the 1745 Jacobite upheaval), but it quickly left the boards, in large part because it contains relatively few lines of political satire.

Rinaldo and Armida

In November or December 1698, Betterton's company staged Dennis's musical drama *Rinaldo and Armida.* Although called on the title page a tragedy, it is now generally considered a dramatic opera. The musical passages were composed by John Eccles, whose contribution Dennis praises in the preface to a separate publication, *The Musical Entertainments in the Tragedy of Rinaldo and Armida.*[3]

The play freely adapts Torquato Tasso's *Gerusalemme Liberata,* first published in 1575 and translated by Edward Fairfax in 1600 as *Jerusalem Delivered.* Tasso shows how during the First Crusade the Christian knight Rinaldo vacillates between carrying out his knightly oaths and succumbing to the pagan enchantress Armida. Dennis's preface and prologue to *Rinaldo and Armida* advertise his intention to develop great, astonishing action, which, as in Sophocles, will produce the great passion of terror. He must alter the characters of Rinaldo and Armida as found in the *Liberata* to achieve a unified tragic effect.

Tasso's Rinaldo is "unequal," that is, inconsistent: "At first he Burns with fierce ambition's fire, / Anon he Dotes like any feeble Squire, / The meer Reverse of all that's noble in Desire."[4] Dennis's Rinaldo acts "Great, with a Solid and real Greatness, very Valiant without Extravagance, and very Human without Weakness." Tasso's Armida, meanwhile, plays the part of a "wanton alluring delicious Creature"; to be tragic, she must act "Proud, Fierce, Stormy, terribly severe" (*Rinaldo,* sigs. a1, a1v, a3v). These two roles were performed by Betterton and Mrs. Barry, who specialized in louder declamatory speeches.

The entire action occurs on a mountain top in the Canaries, either in the enchanted wilderness or at Armida's enchanted palace. Within this setting—"these Isles of Fortune," as Armida describes it—battle two sets of protagonists. On one side argue Urania and two of Rinaldo's friends, Ubaldo and Carlo, who all plead with the hero to return to his martial duty. On the other side, Armida and her supernatural agents invite, cajole, and threaten him to surrender wholly to love. Rinaldo's words and gestures clearly indicate that he internalizes the debate visible on the stage, now yearning for Armida and now ready to leave her. But he always moves closer toward ultimately returning to the field.

Armida from the beginning recognizes Rinaldo's duty to a cause beyond her, so that she obviously engages in a hopeless struggle. Her pride and storminess are revealed emotionally, then, in terms of a violent frustration. She confesses her slavery to love: "The Wildest things are by my pow'r Confin'd: / All but my Wild ungovernable Mind" (*Rinaldo,* 11).

Countering her opponents' arrival, Armida depends mainly upon spirits, who at different times attempt to lull the Christians, enslave the sleeping Rinaldo by frightening him, or simulate universal chaos. Fascinated by the interplay of principle and raw emotion, Dennis is glad to bring his conflict to a logical conclusion: Armida commits suicide while her lover prepares to rejoin her in death on the battlefield.

Dennis designs his scenes to make different passions run one upon another, exciting his audience. Thus praise of the island's beauty gives way to threats, grief, and yearning for glory—all within act 2. Such rhythm works best when lines move to a climax. Strongest in this respect is act 4. Here, after being repelled in act 3 by Rinaldo's "own Reasoning Virtue," Armida's spirits reattack with horribly noisy music. The noise subsides as Rinaldo reaffirms his love while refusing to stay, but then Armida's stabbing herself moves him to a loud "O Grief! O Infinite excess of woe!" (*Rinaldo,* 46).

This dramatic method entails its own limitations, as Dennis

handles it, for his lines between high points too often run prolix. For example, after Ubaldo and Carlo make a Venus and Cupid masque vanish, Rinaldo voices his confusion over four pages. And the exciting stabbing is succeeded by marked anticlimax when a temporarily recovered Armida steps back upon the stage to continue her by now tedious expostulations with Rinaldo.

More pronounced than the tedious lapses are the entertaining mixture and variety of dramatic action with spectacle and Eccles's music. Before Armida's palace—a marginal note reads, *"The Enchanted Palace rises to Musick"*—a shepherd sings a lovely temptation:

> The Jolly Breeze
> That comes whistling through the Trees,
> From all the blissful Region brings
> Perfumes upon its spicy Wings. (*Rinaldo,* 4, 7)

The words and lilting, fast-moving flute music perfectly accent the fragile luxuriance of this fortunate isle.

In contrast, Armida's island spirits' threat to "Heave, Heave up the Crumbling Earth like Moles" is vividly dramatized by "Horrid Musick," thunder, lightning, "Horrible Lyres," chains, howls, and roars (*Rinaldo,* 36–39). The prodigious volume of sound must have rocked the small theater, also known as "Betterton's Booth."

Rinaldo and Armida was not as successful as Aaron Hill's 1711 *Rinaldo* (which offered even more spectacular stage effects), but it did enjoy moderate popularity. A character in a dialogue by John Oldmixon reports seeing the play several times (*CW,* 1:479), and Mrs. Barry states that Betterton's company fared poorly during the 1698–99 season, except for "pretty good success" with Dennis's play.[5] Audiences probably overlooked the tedious passages to enjoy a unified drama featuring some excellent music and entertaining stage business.

Iphigenia

With his blank-verse tragicomedy *Iphigenia,* performed by Betterton's company in December 1699, Dennis turned to subject matter congenial to a classical scholar's interests. Aristotle had used Euripides' *Iphigenia in Tauris* to illustrate technical excellence in plot structure (*Poetics,* 1455a). The new *Iphigenia* seems almost a response to a self-imposed challenge to emulate the structural brilliance of the Greek play. Unfortunately, this in itself is not enough to make good drama.

The preface interestingly sets out the context of the new play. The author fears that his Britain is succumbing to "effeminate Arts" that have corrupted audiences in other nations. He thus will "contribute My Mite towards the being serviceable to the publick," much as he does in his noncritical pamphlets.[6] His service here is to promote the virtue of friendship, which will make viewers more likely to love their country:

> Friendship's the virtue which we recommend,
> He makes a Patriot too who makes a Friend.
> Who freely for his Friend resigns his breath,
> Would for his Country meet a glorious Death.

It is hoped that Euripides' "*Grecian* fire" will "let *English* hearts take flame" (*Iphigenia,* sig. A.2v).

Dennis seems clear about the overall technique needed to produce such a moral effect. He places most emphasis upon his control of the plot, noting that "the Fable or Plot is intirely my own" and "I chiefly took care to form it as regularly as possibly I could, that is, as Reasonably, as Decently, as Greatly, and as Virtuously; and to make it more agreeable, I endeavoured to reconcile Variety to Regularity" (*CW,* 2:389). The basic action comes directly from Euripides: the shipwrecked Orestes meets the priestess Iphigenia, she is to supervise his execution, they discover that they are brother and sister, and they finally return to their homeland. However, Dennis makes two critical changes to carry out his design. First, he replaces King Thoas with an unnamed "Queen of the Scythians." Such a change establishes a love quadrangle involving Iphigenia, Orestes, his friend Pilades, and the Queen, which ultimately points up the strength of true friendship. Second, many elements of mystery, such as the *dea ex machina,* disappear. The strategy here is to convince us that all works logically toward a reasonable and thereby more persuasive conclusion.

An opening exchange between Iphigenia and Euphrosine (a

companion not found in Euripides) reveals that Iphigenia, daughter of Agamemnon and Clytemnestra, escaped a sacrificial death in Argos when a slave died in her place. Iphigenia fled on a ship, only to be shipwrecked upon Scythia, where as priestess at Diana's annual festival she tonight must slay strangers. Unlike Euripides' stern heroine, this lady displays considerable softness:

> My first Request to great *Diana,* is,
> That I may ne'er perform this cruel Function:
> For that which Reason utterly abhors,
> Can ne'er be acceptable to Divinity. (*SW,* 2:17)

In this "regular" play, her softness logically extends into her reaction at seeing the shipwrecked Orestes approach: "Ah Wretch! if thou art by our *Scythians* seen, / Thy business is to die" (*SW,* 2:17).

She and her brother have no idea of one another's presence on the island. Orestes and Pilades are to bring the statue of Diana to Greece and thereby release Orestes from the Furies' wrath. The men at once establish the major theme: "Upon our Virtue then, / Upon our Friendship firmly let's depend, / Immortal Love ne'er stirs a moment from us" (*SW,* 2:19). They return to this theme many times later in the play, often at tiresome length.

Both the Queen and Iphigenia immediately recognize the nobility of the men's friendship and of Orestes' character. In fact, both fall in love with Orestes; he and Pilades meanwhile are both struck by Iphigenia. Numerous complications arise and dissolve: the Queen's troops attack the Greeks, Orestes and Pilades debate as to which should be sacrificed, Iphigenia and the men resolve to escape together, the Queen decides to kill Orestes. Once brother and sister reveal their identities, the action closes speedily: Pilades will wed Iphigenia, Orestes will take the Queen and the statue to Greece, and the sacrifices will end.

As in so much of Dennis's work, a major strength here is the moral firmness. The characters' actions consistently define a clear moral focus from which Dennis never wavers. Orestes and Pilades, for instance, always emphasize their fidelity, and

Iphigenia voices repugnance when the Queen orders Orestes slain (even the Queen soon realizes the injustice). We feel here the same Dennis who elsewhere insists on loyalty to friends and monarch and attacks the intolerance of zealots.

He also capitalizes on sheer technique, relating episodes in aesthetically interesting ways as they multiply. In his version, for example, Orestes' shipwreck bears numerous structural and thematic parallels with Iphigenia's. Characterizations also work logically: because Orestes will not marry the Queen, Iphigenia must kill him, and thus they must meet in an emotionally charged setting right for discovery.

Despite such evidence of skill, the play is not good theater. Overconfidence in that skill mars the effect. The climax in Euripides is Orestes' and Iphigenia's discovery of their feelings and identities. Dennis tries to double the dramatic impact by arranging two discoveries. In act 4 brother and sister rhetorically discover their love:

> ORESTES: When came his [Love's] great Command to you?
> IPHIGENIA: Ev'n now: Attend, and hear his potent Voice!
> ORESTES: Where?
> IPHIGENIA: Here, where amidst Confusion he gives Law.
> ORESTES: Here!
> IPHIGENIA: Here, look and tremble at his Pow'r Divine!
> ORESTES: Ha!
> IPHIGENIA: Is he not manifest? Is he not terrible?
> ORESTES: Oh Astonishment! (*SW*, 2:70)

This stichomythic format works to a degree, but Dennis loses much effect by overextending the device through nearly two hundred lines. In his preface he notes that "upon *Orestes* discovering his passion to *Iphigenia* in the fourth Act, there ran a general Murmur through the Pit, which is what I had never seen before" (*CW*, 2:390). Perhaps the audience marveled at his invention; perhaps they felt both marvel and tedium. The final "surprise" comes as an anticlimax, for during act 5 they must sit through much the same thing.

The lines have no stylistic vibrancy. As H. D. F. Kitto argues, Euripides keeps his plot moving with a sense of light engagement

proper to tragicomedy.[7] Dennis, in contrast, tends toward un-
leavened soberness, turgidity, and drawing out. Instead of making a dramatic point quickly and moving on, he often draws
out a point through dozens of listless lines such as Pilades':

> I attempted to regain that Liberty,
> Of which your Pow'r unjustly had depriv'd me.
> What Reason could you find, insulting Queen,
> To make them Captives whom the Gods made free,
> And gave them Souls deserving Liberty?
> As against Nature's Laws we are your Victims,
> Against the Right of Nations we're your Captives;
> And any way was lawful to fair Liberty,
> Which we were born for, and for which we'll die.
>
> > (*SW*, 2:59)

Attempts at "poetic" fire are unrelievedly loud, as when Orestes
roars:

> Dost thou not see th'inexorable Fury?
> Look how her bloody Mouth spouts purple Foam,
> And her black Nostrils, Cataracts of Fire!
> Gods! how her cruel Eyes shoot Horrors thro my Soul!
>
> > (*SW*, 2:29)

Also lacking in Dennis is the poet's wonder at mystery found
in Euripides. Gone are Orestes' madness, the miraculous explanation of Iphigenia's transport to Tauris, and the *dea ex machina,*
all expressed in exciting language. In their place are flat, rea-
soned arguments hopefully more appropriate for a Restoration
audience, but actually not entertaining to any audience.

When the author claims, "The general success of the following
Poem has been neither despicable nor extraordinary," he sounds
unsure for a man usually certain of his verdict (*Iphigenia,* sig.
A.1v). To be sure, Theophilus Cibber finds "this by far the
most affecting tragedy of our author; it is almost impossible
to read it without tears," while Kippis judges it "pathetic and
interesting."[8] But others are less generous.

Many focus on the turgidity, the "Tremendous" lines (even
Cibber qualifies his praise with "though it abounds with bom-
bast"), the dwindling audiences. John Downes reports that the

play "answer'd not the Expences they were at in Cloathing it"[9]; others note simply its being damned. The most interesting response is Abel Boyer's explanation for the failure of his own *Iphigenia in Aulis:* "This Tragedy came out upon the Neck of another of the same Name, which being the product of a *Giant-Wit,* and a *Giant-Critick* . . . had miserably balk'd the World's Expectation; and most People having been tir'd at *Lincoln's-Inn-Fields,* did not care to venture their Patience at *Drury-lane,* upon a false Supposition that the two *Iphigenia's* were much alike."[10]

Dennis's audience doubtless felt what we feel: despite the announced patriotic intention, Dennis really has not justified all his work in adapting Euripides.[11]

Liberty Asserted

On 24 February 1704 Little Lincoln's-Inn-Fields premiered Dennis's most successful play, *Liberty Asserted.* This tragedy enjoyed a total of ten performances during its first run, followed by revivals in 1707 and 1746.

Dennis relished the success, because in *Liberty Asserted* he applies most consciously his doctrine that "the Instructions which we receive from the Stage ought to be for the Benefit of the lawful establish'd Government" (*CW*, 1:320).[12] Since his European tour he had been espousing liberty and one's obligation to improve his society while remaining true to himself, and warning of the threat posed by Louis XIV to Englishmen's freedom. *Liberty Asserted* demonstrates how in a primitive setting one can learn these "Instructions" by being forced into a moral dilemma.

The scene is the Iroquoian nation of Angie, in Canada, site of warfare between the Iroquois with their English allies and the Hurons with their French allies. Ulamar, the heroic Angian leader, has conquered his enemies, who now sue for peace. His English friend Beaufort and other counselors warn that the treacherous French will attack again if he grants them their terms. However, Ulamar's mother, Sakia, knows that she can rejoin her Huron people and French husband only if Ulamar grants these terms. Listening to her threats of suicide, he relents and approves the treaty.

Meanwhile, Ulamar and Beaufort have both sought the hand

of the Iroquois princess Irene. As in *Iphigenia,* both young men feel conflict between friendship and self-interest, which parallels and emphasizes the larger dilemma in the main plot. Irene's father gives her to Ulamar, much to Sakia's displeasure.

Ulamar and Irene cannot enjoy their wedding night, for the French take advantage of the truce and launch a surprise attack in which Irene's father dies. After being captured, Ulamar quickly converts the valiant Frenchman Miramont to the side of England and liberty. With the aid of Miramont and much incredible luck, Ulamar escapes the death sentence ordered by the French general Frontenac when Sakia discovers that Frontenac and Ulamar are father and son. The play concludes as Frontenac miraculously sheds the "Lethargick Dream" of French slavery and joins his family and the friends of "Godlike Liberty" (*SW,* 2:194).

No one can miss Dennis's point. The audience hear many times that they are "fair Supports of Liberty . . . against a faithless Race." The English-Iroquois forces seem incredibly noble, the French morally no better than "rank and filthy Weeds" (*SW,* 2:113, 111). In the final scene Ulamar directly warns us:

> Never to sacrifice the publick Good
> Either to foreign, or to home-bred Tyrants,
> For the vile Interest of themselves and Families;
> For that upon their Families and selves
> Brings certain Ruin.
>
> (*SW,* 2:198)

Dennis observes in the preface that he has "been accus'd of repeating the same thing in the Play, the Prologue and Epilogue," and now the preface (*CW,* 1:321). This sort of repetition of one's didactic message is not likely to excite modern readers; however, after a while we can find ourselves looking forward to Dennis's next vividly phrased contrast of the heroes and the villains. The sharp verbal attacks against Louis, along with Dennis's pride in his play, led to more than one apocryphal story. One such tale has Dennis trembling in fear of Gallic retaliation and begging the Duke of Marlborough to protect him.[13]

The players have some fine opportunities to show dramatic flair. In particular, Sakia feels torn by "various Furies in my Soul" as she pleads for Ulamar to make the decision that she knows he abhors, attempts suicide, and joyfully discovers her husband. Dennis commends Mrs. Barry's handling of the role, for "that incomparable Actress changing like Nature which she represents, from Passion to Passion, from Extream to Extream, with piercing Force, and with easie Grace, changes the Hearts of all who see her with irresistible Pleasure" (*CW,* 1:324). Such acting exactly fits Dennis's conception of how to agitate passions in art. We likewise hear in one passage that Irene (played by Mrs. Bracegirdle) grieves with despair in her eyes, dying accents, and overflowing eyes. Frontenac also physically intimates his upcoming change of allegiance by wincing at the mention of his son and confessing, "Thou wilt melt me to my Ruin" (*SW,* 2:170).

The most astounding character is Ulamar, through the early acts the perfect, always victorious martial hero "sent express from Heav'n." A spokesman for human liberty, he views his military prowess within a broader human context:

> For ever blest be that eternal Pow'r
> That gave me a human comprehensive Soul,
> That can look down upon all narrow Principles.
> For every brave Man's Country is the Universe,
> His Countrymen Mankind. . . .
>
> (*SW,* 2:127)

This abstract thinking closely matches that found in Dennis's other statements against intolerance, as in *The Reverse.* Fortunately, Ulamar also acts like a real human being when he has to make impossible moral choices and realizes his nearly fatal mistake: "I poorly ran the Hazard of my Country / To save my House, and on my House the first, / The greatest, and most dismal Vengeance falls" (*SW,* 2:172).

Liberty Asserted has weaknesses that disqualify it as a major play. It shows a flamboyance of diction aptly satirized by Henry Fielding in *The Tragedy of Tragedies* (1731). It presents fantastic incidents and characterization. And in its direct teaching of Lockean and Whig principles of liberty, it is "perhaps the most calculated attempt to dramatize political ideology" during Queen Anne's reign. This last characteristic Addison senses when he notes that the play "has yᵉ Whiggs for its patrons and Supporters."[14]

Yet the play is still readable. Even today, the right cast of players could certainly bring out something of melodrama, more of the passionate vicissitudes resulting from clashing priorities. Dennis has found the right conflict of the right ideas for him to write the aesthetically strongest play of his career. That *Liberty Asserted* is not so major as several of his nondramatic works indicates simply that drama is not his forte.

Gibraltar

Giles Jacob felt some confusion while editing material for his capsule biography of Dennis: "In the Account this Gentleman sent, he omitted, but for what Reason is unknown to us, a Play wrote by him, call'd, *Gibraltar*. . . ."[15] This play, a farcical romantic comedy, failed utterly in its 16 and 20 February 1705 performances at Drury Lane. In his preface Dennis sadly recounts the disaster: unspecified "Calamities" destroyed the rehearsal, during the first performance the play "was not suffer'd to be heard," and on the final night it was poorly acted (*CW*, 1:380). We should add to this list the play's inferior quality.

The comedy has topical reference, being set in a village near Gibraltar, which the English had recently captured. Wilmot and Vincent, two young English colonels, have been imprisoned by the French and are now ransomed. They plot to win Leonora and Jacquelinda, nieces of the tyrannical Diego, a Spanish captain. With the aid of Wilmot's servant Fetcher, Diego's assistant, and the girls' duenna Blincarda, they work on the captain's greed to secure their aim. The ladies simultaneously plot to test and win the young men's love. Darkness and disguises (Diego and Blincarda exchange dress as the sisters pretend to be soldiers) combine with the excitement over the English victory to facilitate the mutual plotting. Diego at last finds himself tricked into approving the two marriages and giving his nieces their inheritances.

Gibraltar exhibits few high points. In rare moments Dennis produces clever phrasings to show the ladies' intriguingly fast wit. In one such passage they discuss their progress:

> LEONORA: We have pelted one another these Three Weeks with the Artillery of our Eyes.
>
> JACQUELINDA: That's but Small Shot. But now the Colonels are drawing down their Great Guns upon us.[16]

Unfortunately, the norm proves to be awkwardness, wordiness, and emptiness.

A mariner rambles, "I am no Wordy-Man, do you see— Wordy-Men are Knaves, and most an end Cowards to boot too; do you see, a Man of Words and not of Deeds," etc. Leonora carries on about love in empty, fashionable love banter: "Let him enslave me, so he Lov'd me! I had rather owe my Confinement to his Amorous Jealousie, than my Freedom to his dull Indifference. The Woman is Impudent, who pretends to Love, and complains of her Confinement, to him whom she pretends to Love." And a corporal pretends to be Irish in a silly, dispensable ethnic parody: "I by my shoul will we. For we well cut Tat shweet Troat of thine, and then we will make howl upon dy body, unless thou dost ush more shevil fraashis ub ub ub ub ou" (*Gibraltar,* 44, 34, 63). Dennis tries many kinds of jokes, but most of the writing sounds barely professional.

Arthur Bedford in *The Evil and Danger of Stage-Plays* (1706) rightly assesses another major weakness in the play, its questionable morality. The many jokes about buying and seducing women, sexual puns, jests about drunkenness, and profane oaths fully document Bedford's charge. We question Dennis's moral vision when his heroines shout, "Hell and Confusion!" and a servant gains admiration by arguing that men should drink in Spain, where the wine is good and the harlots execrable, and whore in London, "where the Wenches are Good and Cheap, and Tax-free" (*Gibraltar,* 6).

Although Dennis has many chances to give us real substance, he lacks here the wholeness of vision to pursue deeper meanings. His characters at times voice his favorite sentiments of devotion to country and liberty, but he quickly drops such thoughts. Strangely, as if to rectify what he has left undone, Dennis ends with an afterthought foreign to the tone of the action as a captain tells Wilmot, "The Intelligence which we receiv'd from you, and the Service which you have done the Publick, have produc'd the happy consequence of helping you to so charming a Creature" (*Gibraltar*, 78).

Dennis misses opportunities for character development and poetry. The money-hungry Diego could share much with Jonson's Volpone and his dupes, but Dennis leaves his Don a flat stereotype. We see much of nighttime delusions and disguises but find no poetic exploration of such ideas as change of identity, as are found in *A Midsummer Night's Dream.*

Robert Hume feels that "Dennis does passably . . . but the results are a bit heavy for so trivial a confection."[17] Dennis in neither telling Jacob about the play nor reprinting it obviously feels less sure than Hume about its merits. Having noted in the prologue that he has "lately Sung a loftier strain" in his Blenheim poem, Dennis upon later reflection has decided that his dramatic "Trifle" violates his most deeply felt principles concerning the aesthetic and moral ends of drama.

Appius and Virginia

Most readers know *Appius and Virginia* only by the footnote to Pope's reference to Appius in *An Essay on Criticism.* Actually, this is one of Dennis's best plays, certainly a better one than *Gibraltar* and "The Masque of Orpheus and Euridice" (published in the February 1707 *Muses Mercury*), a brief composition notable for little beyond its reproducing the noise of *Rinaldo and Armida.* Usually a hasty writer, Dennis expended much labor over his tragedy. In October 1707 he is busy writing "that Raskal Appius," and almost a year later he has completed only four acts (*OL,* 1:129, 115). This care produced at best a moderate success, the drama premiering on 5 February 1709 and running four nights. But it also produced a respectable play.[18]

Dennis uses material from Livy and Dionysius of Halicarnassus, to which he adds much of his own invention. Set in Rome of 450 B.C., the play describes the climactic villainy and downfall of Appius Claudius, one of the decemvirs chosen to replace the tribunes while the statutes are being rewritten. Appius has perverted the temporary arrangement to assume despotic control.

Lucius Icilius and fellow patriots rage over the tyrant's atrocities, particularly his assassination of a popular military leader and his repeated attempts to win Virginia, who is betrothed to Icilius. The patriots have the chance to kill Appius when he visits Virginia, but she helps him escape when he feigns repentance. Appius next attempts to win her within his own court by decreeing her a slave to one of his followers. He sentences to death not only Icilius and his friends but his own uncle Claudius, who in defending both the honor of his family and Virginia's rights has accused Appius of criminality. Her father, Virginius, maintains her purity by killing her. Just then we hear that all Roman sectors are rebelling against Appius, whom Icilius slays. Plans for revenge against the remaining decemvirs are postponed as Icilius and Virginius prepare to join the other newly chosen tribunes.

Despite his heroic behavior, Icilius arouses little interest. He is the stereotyped hero who must do brave things against a tyrant. He tries to make Romans throw off their "Lethargick Slumber" and defend their rights, he fights well, he worries about Virginia, and he nobly hurls accusations at his enemy. Yet we always feel that he is doing merely what we expect of him.

Virginia (about whom Dennis found little in his sources) is more complicated and interesting. She early seems a neophyte at the business of life. We first see her trembling at the mention of Appius and confessing, "My Heart is form'd of such a tender Mold, / I ne'er could see the vilest Creature die" (*SW,* 2:224). Her innate tenderness and inexperience lead immediately to her fatal blunder of letting the incensed Appius escape. She learns quickly, however, for she later attacks him for his misdeeds and refuses all inducements, showing the firm spirit of true Roman (and English) women in her defense of moral virtue, which "must last when *Rome* shall be no more" (*SW,* 2:260). Her death by Virginius's hand implies much more than a young innocent's sacrifice, as father and daughter both understand:

> VIRGINIUS: Oh! thus thy Father vindicates thy Freedom,
> And thus secures thy Virtue: Tyrant, Tyrant,
> Thus with the sprinkling of this sacred Blood,
> I consecrate thee to the infernal Powers.

VIRGINIA: I am free;
            And *Rome,* that will its Freedom owe to me,
            Upon the Wings of her victorious Eagles
            Shall thro all Times and Places bear my Virtue:
            I die a *Roman* now. . . .

                                    (*SW,* 2:276–77)

In his optimistic hope that the gods "Have chosen thee the
glorious Instrument / Of freeing *Rome,*" Icilius has not guessed
the tragic depth to which his beloved can define her mission
(*SW,* 2:224).

For sheer entertaining villainy, Dennis never outdoes his characterization of Appius. Unbound by laws made by himself or
the gods, this tyrant will do anything to control "the base Scum"
who gave him power. And he will even destroy his political
future to rape Virginia. Everyone of note despises him: the
patriots call him a haughty nighttime thief, Claudius finds him
an inhumane degenerate, and Virginia notes the insane cruelty
in "his sparkling bloody Eyes." But Dennis also gets inside
his villain to emphasize the emotional imbalance that produces
his downfall. Appius's "detested Passion" for Virginia, which
has overcome his "feeble Reason," constantly torments him.
We thus have not a stock villain but a human being who writhes:
"For O I rave! I rave! a raging Fever / Shakes my tempestuous
Frame, devours my Blood, / And scorches and consumes my
inmost Marrow" (*SW,* 2:247–48).

Appius and Virginia must be judged a very loud play. One
shouted horrific begets another as characters threaten, plead,
cajole, and slay. Persuading Virginia of his penitence, Appius
describes his vision of Hell:

> Millions of Ghosts, that star'd with stony Eyes,
> And gnash'd with Iron Teeth, I there beheld
> Toss'd from the Banks, amidst the flaming Gold,
> And plung'd by red-hot Prongs of snaky Furies.
>   (*SW,* 2:232)

Horrors, bleeding ghosts, ghastly precipices, raging seas, and
thunder fill the pages. Even Appius's final groan is celebrated
with the noise of "Attend ye Furies, / Attend ye skreaming

Ghosts of murder'd *Romans"* (*SW,* 2:285). Dennis is surely attempting to rouse tragic passions; he also numbs our ears.

The play's first critics pass over the intended moral, that just vengeance will make us respect celestial laws, to focus on the loud style. John Gay in *The Mohocks* ridicules Dennis by inventing a subject *"Horrid* and *Tremendous."* And his dialogue parodies Dennis's in its wondrously mad fustian: "By all the Elements, and all the Powers, / Celestial, nay Terrestrial, and Infernal; / By *Acheron,* and the black Streams of *Styx.* . . ."[19] Pope probably invented the story that Dennis, who had devised a new way to make thunder to underscore the louder speeches in the play, shouted upon hearing thunder during the performance of someone else's play, "S'death! that is *my* Thunder."[20] Actually, the style contributes to the positive effect of *Appius and Virginia;* Dennis unfortunately overdoes it. In terms of character portrayal and the defense of personal liberty, the play achieves a good deal.

The Shakespearean Adaptations

The Comical Gallant.   Dennis's nadir in theatrical writing comes with *The Comical Gallant: or The Amours of Sir John Falstaffe,* performed and published in the spring of 1702. This comedy is the only adaptation of *The Merry Wives of Windsor* to be staged during the first half of the eighteenth century. However, the original enjoyed great popularity, as did the Falstaff of the Henry IV plays, so that in terms of audience receptivity to the material being adapted, Dennis's timing seems right.

To begin to see what goes awry, we might briefly consider several points in *A Large Account of the Taste in Poetry, and the Causes of the Degeneracy of It,* the epistle dedicatory attached to *The Comical Gallant.* Dennis feels convinced that Shakespeare's play deserves a revival, first because it originally had· royal sanction, Queen Elizabeth demanding its composition (Dennis is the first to record this tradition). The Falstaff of *The Merry Wives,* moreover, is a better dramatic character than the Falstaff in *1 Henry IV*—a verdict unlikely to find many adherents today— because here he engages in action, which "is the business of the Stage" (*CW,* 1:280).

However, two problems caused by Shakespeare's hasty writ-

ing, Dennis argues, weaken *The Merry Wives.* First, the three
main lines of action are too many; second, speeches often sound
too affected for comedy. The remedies appropriately involve
structure and style: Dennis will unify the action by centering
all on Fenton's marriage, and he will make the dialogue freer
and easier, so that it will befit the common status of the play's
characters.

Dennis goes into further detail about such points as his alterations of four scenes, the emphasis upon humor (not wit) because
it develops action, the use of low characters in comedy, and
the necessity that humor both delight us and expose our follies.
He concludes with several pages on debased theatrical taste,
which, along with the incompetent performance of the Falstaff
role, turned the audience against his play.

A close recounting of the plot is unnecessary, since for the
most part Dennis follows Shakespeare rather closely, and several
scholars have carefully noted the scene-by-scene changes made
by Dennis.[21] We still have the braggart Falstaff vainly trying
to woo married ladies, the jealous Ford ready to test his wife's
fidelity, the young lovers Fenton and Ann hoping to outwit
their elders, and the resolution in Windsor Park.

Dennis's attempt to unify the plot by making all action contribute to the wedding plans of Fenton and Ann does not produce
outstanding results, for this change is in effect merely cosmetic.
In act 1 Fenton tells the Host of the Garter Inn and Ann that
through his machinations Falstaff will believe Mrs. Ford and
Mrs. Page both in love with the old knight, and their husbands
will learn of Falstaff's amorous designs. The resulting chaos is
to camouflage the young people's elopement. We see nothing
more of Fenton until his return late in act 4, when he does
little except to remind us of how well his plot is working. He
seems only a weak cousin of the young plotters who add so
much to the intrigue comedies of Wycherley and Congreve.
Meanwhile, all our attention has focused on Falstaff's blundering
relations with the wives and Ford. Thus, we do not feel the
kind of unity described in *A Large Account.* Rather, the Fenton-
Ann plot line is even more subordinate than in the original.

A far more pronounced change sees Ford, not Falstaff, receiving the most severe punishment. This alteration greatly damages
the conclusion, where Ford now suffers the fairies' pinches and

candle burns. His pain becomes fully distasteful as the torture proceeds throughout a song, far longer than Shakespeare's, sadistically concluding, "Now laugh at his Woe, / And as he cries Oh— / Reply with a He, Ho, Hi, Ho."[22] Although Falstaff is admonished, Ford suffers extreme public humiliation as he confesses, "I had been such an Ass, and so vilely wrong'd the very best of Women" (*Comical Gallant*, 45).

Dennis has obviously reworked the comic plot to instruct us about our folly, but at what a price! We have lost all the richness Shakespeare creates when he puts Falstaff into a ritualistic scapegoat role.[23] All that the patched-together Shakespearean passages add up to is a sterile exemplum.

Also weak are Dennis's stylistic changes. Many puns that reinforce the vitality and imaginative playfulness of the original simply disappear. For instance, the Falstaff who has just been dumped into the Thames in a basket seems far less blustering when he does not quibble, "Mistress Ford? I have had ford enough. I was thrown into the ford; I have my belly full of ford."[24]

Or, probably making sure that all points are clear, Dennis often extends passages needlessly. At the very end of *The Merry Wives,* Mrs. Page steers everyone toward the exits with "let us every one go home, / And laugh this sport o'er by a country fire— / Sir John and all."[25] Dennis totally eradicates this parting sense of rural magic by giving us several passages that explain fully who acquires particular bits of wisdom.

We find additions perhaps designed to emphasize the low status of characters—but most surely also to entertain the audience. Several new sections of farce (such as the scuffle as act 4 opens) put more action into the play, although Shakespeare might seem to have enough action already. The most outrageous addition comes in act 2. Falstaff mistakenly tries to whet the disguised Ford's sexual appetite for Mrs. Ford but succeeds only in convincing Ford of his cuckoldom. As lines explicitly detail how she bares herself—Hazelton Spencer labels the dialogue "unquotable"[26]—Ford feels pain foreshadowing that to be felt in act 5. If he expects us to find such lines humorous, Dennis has misgauged our relish for low comedy.

Dennis's critics have proven anything but kind to *The Comical Gallant.* A contemporary wit observes, "So much as was *Shake-*

spear's was lik'd, but all his own damn'd, and for his sake the whole Play soon afterwards." Others have found it "a very indifferent Alteration," "a vicious alteration," and a "shocking travesty." One irate scholar judges it "a contemptible compound of farce and smut. . . . the play died immediately; and if any one but the adapter mourned, I have not seen the record of it."[27]

Granted, Dennis faced some unusual problems beyond his control. The stage was still under attack by Jeremy Collier and other moralists, during most of March and April theaters remained closed because of King William's death, and Dennis could not choose the actor to play his comic lead. *The Comical Gallant,* however, could not under the best of circumstances please an audience.

The Invader of His Country. Dennis ended his career as dramatist with *The Invader of His Country: or, The Fatal Resentment.* Although written in 1710, this adaptation of *Coriolanus* did not see performance until 1719 or publication until the following year. Dennis refers to recently active Jacobites in his prologue:

> For as when *Britain*'s Rebel Sons of late
> Combin'd with Foreign Foes t'invade the State,
> She to your [audience's] Valour and your Conduct owes,
> That she subdued and crush'd her num'rous Foes:[28]

Clearly, like Shakespeare, Nahum Tate, and others who had taken up the Coriolanus story, Dennis is trying to take advantage of latent political implications.

As in his alteration of *The Merry Wives,* Dennis here retains most of Shakespeare's action while changing the relationships of the characters, rethinking the strategies of scenes, and greatly changing the final act. We still have the noble Caius Martius Coriolanus, who successfully leads the Romans against the Volscians, assumes the name "Coriolanus," is banished because of his disdain for the Roman populace, leads the Volscians against Rome, and dies within Rome. But the alterations create a markedly different play.

Dennis's comments elsewhere on *Coriolanus* reveal his own discomfort with Shakespeare's writing. According to the *Essay* on Shakespeare, the characters of Aufidius and Menenius, the treatment of Coriolanus, and the lack of "celestial Fire" all cry out for a new version of *Coriolanus*. His solution overall gives us drama more unified, clearer, and less disturbing: more sensible perhaps, but also less rewarding.

The working of this sensibleness is evident in the revision of Shakespeare's act 1, which to Dennis exhibits a fearful lack of unity. He cannot see how the switches among the Roman citizens and Coriolanus, Aufidius in Corioles, Coriolanus's mother and wife in Rome, and battle scenes can make sense to the typical audience of his day. George C. Branam rightly suggests that in Dennis's mind "the eighteenth-century audience," during opening scenes, "preferred clarity and simplicity of pattern, and was likely to be impatient of threads of action that could not be related easily and swiftly to what had gone before."[29]

The new act 1 very simply begins in the middle of the battle and takes us straightforwardly to the Roman victory. Completely missing now are the women's troubled exchange and all other disruptions in the continuity. Such revision makes intellectual good sense, but at the same time we must sacrifice much of Shakespeare's complexity: the early hints that without the citizens' full support Coriolanus is acting the hero in isolation, the mystifying power of a woman (Volumnia) over the man performing marvelous feats, the nervous energy deriving from fast scene changes, the overriding sense that events are not so simple as the hero may wish.

Dennis tries to normalize characters' personalities and their relations to one another, to unclutter feelings. Prime examples are the drastically changed roles of Coriolanus's mother and his wife. Before his triumphant return to Rome, they sound much as they do in *Coriolanus*, Volumnia relishing her son's martial prowess and Virgilia uneasy about his safety. However, upon his entrance, we find a total rearrangement. Saying nothing, Shakespeare's Virgilia seems little more than an onlooker. Cominius first says, "Look, sir, your mother"; Coriolanus kneels before Volumnia; and she reminds him, "But O, thy wife!"[30] In contrast, the passage in *The Invader of His Country* begins with Virgilia's impetuous lines of "fierce Convulsions of transporting Joy!" wherein it is now she who reminds Coriolanus, "But see, the noblest Mother of the World / Remains too long neglected." To this he responds, "I knew not till this Moment she was here" (*Invader*, 16).

Likewise, when Coriolanus is banished, Shakespeare gives Virgilia only four words, Volumnia several strong lines. Dennis, in contrast, gets Volumnia off the stage with "I leave thee to *Virgilia*, / She has most need of Comfort," upon which ensues a tearful scene as "my dear *Virgilia*" sobs with grief and her husband shudders, "Adieu! / In quest of great Revenge thy Lover flies" (*Invader*, 43–45). Dennis is striving to establish a more recognizably normal relationship between man and wife, one in which wife comes before mother.

This particular kind of change is one way in which Dennis makes the most important "improvement," the simplification of Coriolanus. More noticeably, Dennis expands his heroic stature. Everyone refers to him as "Substitute of *Jove*," "Godlike Man," or "a God," while his foes sink "in Adoration." But he is a man-god too proud to listen to the populace and ready to pursue his vision to his own destruction. Dennis omits almost everything that might compromise this easily recognized type of hero. Gone, for instance, is the fine stroke of Coriolanus's not freeing his aged benefactor simply because he cannot recall the man's name. Gone is the careful attention to the emotional import of names in his mind, as seen in his crazed response to Aufidius's taunting words "traitor," "Martius," and "boy." Gone, as we have seen, is the mama's-boy syndrome. Dennis thus removes nasty or irrational traits to make the man more identifiable and deserving of our sympathy. But in so doing, he produces a one-dimensional and uninteresting superhero.

We should also note Dennis's rehandling of the very end of the play. He discards the richness and incredible speed of events felt when Shakespeare's Aufidius (whose own motives are complex) spurs the conspirators to their climactic "Kill, kill, kill, kill, kill him!" Coriolanus falls, and the emotionally spent Aufidius honors Coriolanus and helps carry him off—all in two dozen lines. Also gone is the sense of this hero's place within society. As one critic observes of Shakespeare's final lines, "Only Coriolanus is dead; the community will go on, in the endless tragicomic cycle of regeneration, devouring the heroes it nurtures and immortalizes because it is in its nature to do so."[31] The drawing of such implications tells us that Shakespeare has probed the emotional depths of social consciousness as well as of the troubled, alienated hero.

But, again, Dennis avoids what he feels only muddles the point of the drama. Disturbed at Aufidius's not receiving his due punishment, he wreaks poetic justice by having Coriolanus kill Aufidius and several tribunes, only to be stabbed from behind, indicating that perfidy will beget perfidy. Bodies take some time to fall, to the accompaniment of speeches and offstage shrieks. Then Volumnia and Virgilia proclaim conventional grief at length, and finally, well over a hundred lines after the first stabbing, Cominius tells us directly not to conspire with foreign powers and betray our native land.

Dennis has made sure that we cannot possibly miss his intention by simplifying his characters and the action. But the result is flat, untrue to life, and dull. *The Invader of His Country* seems competent, but we again wonder whether it was worth doing. In the dedication and elsewhere, Dennis blames the play's brief run upon the Drury Lane managers' postponing its production. We must admit, however, that although this adaptation is superior to *The Comical Gallant,* it probably would have had little more success given better timing.

Chapter Five

Poetry

Earliest Verse of a Young Gentleman

Much of Dennis's earlier verse was first published here and there and has little value. In 1692, for example, several poems appeared in the *Gentleman's Journal*, Peter Motteux's entertaining medley of current news, queries and answers, verse epistles, amorous ditties, odes, fables, enigmas, social essays, accounts of recent books, music, and much else. Dennis's poetic contributions include his solution to an enigma submitted by Nahum Tate; translations of Boileau, Juvenal, and Horace; burlesque verses, "Upon Our Victory at Sea," and social verses. All of the poems were later published in Dennis's own volumes.

Witty poems.   Most of this early poetry is a conscious, unsuccessful attempt to become known as a witty gentleman. The completeness of the failure seems most obvious when we read *Poems in Burlesque,* twenty-two pages of rough comic verse published in 1692. The seven poems achieve the tumbling, madcap tone of most Restoration burlesques, which one writer likens to a "wanton Chamber-maid, with her Petticoats tuck'd up, in her Masque and Pattens, who walks, runs, stumbles, stops, looks about, and laughs, and perhaps all in less than a Minute."[1] Unfortunately, this tone of itself cannot give poetry lasting value.

The observation that Fleetwood Shepherd, the book's dedicatee, "ner'e gave Gods or Men offence, / By off'ring . . . Truth and Sense" prepares us for nonsense.[2] And nonsense we get. In "The Story of *Orpheus* Burlesqu'd," the best of the seven poems, Orpheus does not care for Eurydice, so he schemes to make her remain in Hell. The final lines celebrate, "He Singing thus, repass'd the Ferry, / Since Spouse is damn'd I will be merry" (*Poems in Burlesque,* 17). This burlesque seems a classical scholar's toying with material that he has long enjoyed.

Much more doubtful in tone are the other poems in the collection. "An Explication of Mr. *Tate's Riddle*" cleverly discusses the puppet Punchinello, but the whole effort is a waste of time. The most substantial couplet describes the "*Swiss* wond'ring to hear *Puppet* squeak, / And see him frisk with Faiery Freak." Other poems are cynical, mean, and often obscene. According to "A Days Ramble in *Covent-Garden,*" church is "Where Virgins Counterfeit and Stale, / Are daily in Rows expos'd to Sale" (*Poems in Burlesque,* 22, 11). A poem upon a Scottish parson finds his daughter losing control of her bladder as she laughs at his sermons, and a tavern brawl between three womanizing sots and the wife of one of them features a chamber pot slopping its contents down the poor fellow's head.

Although Dennis composes rollicking octosyllabic lines and creates amusing rhymes such as "Choler"–"maul her" and "Euridice"–"Eye did see," *Poems in Burlesque* has no lasting value. One scholar, finding Dennis's prose better than his verse, believes him to focus too much here on "curious or misshapen characters copied from life" to achieve real significance. Perhaps more helpful is another critic's feeling that worthwhile burlesque like *Hudibras* establishes "a conflict between a farcical benevolent comedy and a satirical moral and philosophical intention."³ *Poems in Burlesque* involves a much leaner combination of farce and satiric meanness; there is no sense of benevolence or philosophical depth. It is pure entertainment, as Hooker suggests, a mere trifle (*CW,* 2:x).

Fables. More amenable to Dennis's temperament, although still not spectacular poetry, are the ten animal fables in the 1693 *Miscellanies.* Between 1650 and 1750 the fable, a short didactic narrative usually featuring animal characters, enjoyed great popularity. Jean de La Fontaine, Roger L'Estrange, John Dryden, John Gay, Jonathan Swift, Matthew Prior, and others contributed much to a vigorous tradition. Dennis joins numerous minor poetic talents in using the tradition to compose some entertaining verse, but he adds little to it.

Locke and almost everyone else who during the seventeenth or eighteenth century discusses the fable point out its usefulness as a didactic tool. Dennis makes much of this use: "For as when *AEsop* introduces a Horse, or a Dog, or a Wolf, or a Lion, he does not pretend to shew us any singular Animal, but only to shew the Nature of that Creature. . . . every true Dramatick

Poem is a Fable as much as any one of *AEsop*'s; it has in its
Nature a direct Tendency to teach moral Virtue" (*CW*, 2:308).
The *Gentleman's Journal* praises Dennis for producing fables "at
least equal to the Originals of a Master who was once reputed
inimitable. To those merry Fables he hath given us grave Morals,
which will make them at least as instructive as pleasant. For,
as you know, Fables . . . are Paths fill'd with Roses, that lead
us to the knowledge of Virtue more agreeably. . . ."⁴ An overall problem, however, lies in the great disparity between this
emphasis on instruction and the burlesque comic technique used
to make the instruction pleasurable.

Dennis does not go directly to Aesop for his material. Rather,
although he never tells us so, he is publishing the first English
translations of poems from La Fontaine's immensely popular
Fables. A fast glance at La Fontaine's verses and then at Dennis's
reveals differences great enough to make the English versions
seem loose adaptations in contrast to the much closer translations
found in Mandeville's *AEsop Dress'd.*⁵ Essentially, Dennis replaces La Fontaine's elegant wit with the thumping burlesque
humor of Samuel Butler, and he expands the moral tag on each
fable.

The action parts of Dennis's versions depict the animals as
anything but dignified and restrained, as they usually are in
La Fontaine. Thus the pig in "The *Pig,* the *Goat,* and the *Sheep*"
illustrates the futility of foreseeing one's dismal end. He
screeches in panic that he is one

> Whom Wastcoateer has made a Fat Pig,
> For some Cits ravenous Spouse, with Brat big.
> 'Tis for her maw I'm grown this Squab bit;
> May the Jade choak with the first gobbet.⁶

Modish diction like "Cits," the fast octosyllabic lines, the femi-
nine rhymes, and the lowly self-image vividly show a fool in
action. Such merciless downgrading of the animal hero may
provide some entertainment, but we encounter a problem of
tone. Hudibrastic burlesque presupposes a wide gap between
a highly dignified topic and its low comic treatment to produce
mental sparks. Little such distance exists with the lowly pig,
so that here the comedy does not have great power.

In the moral concluding each fable, Dennis makes certain that we recognize the maxim. His favorite procedure is to present the action and then in the moral go into implications at considerable length. For instance, "of the *Aunt* [*sic*] and the *Grasshopper*" concludes with a moral nearly as long as the main section. In contrast to what we find in that opening section, the lines are now heroic couplets, the tone is noncomic didacticism, and the treatment is abstract. Through the twenty-eight lines we are wittily advised through repetitive arguments to live before age extinguishes joy and to beware of becoming a drudge like the ant. In other pages a concluding moral may be far longer than its opening action. In fact, "The *Lyon* and the *Ass* a Hunting" not only contains a five-section moral but is followed by a lengthy independent poem, "Some Moral Reflections Concerning Vanity, Written upon the Occasion of Burlesquing the Fable of the *Ass* and the *Lyon*," which could easily be reduced by half.

Dennis has thought carefully about fable writing, and his versions are more able than many others, but he does not fully succeed. We can sense an unresolved conflict between what Dennis sees as hack wit writing and literature of more serious intent. He tries but cannot get where he wishes to go with this poetic vehicle.

Polite verse. Little need be said about Dennis's handful of social poems, which read like a young gallant's calling card. Most of this verse we find in the *Miscellanies* and the *Gentleman's Journal* but not in later publications. "To Sylvia" never was published in a Dennis book, appearing instead in the *Gentleman's Journal* and in the Duke of Buckingham's *Chorus Poetarum.* Only one poem, "To a Painter," did Dennis see fit to include in *The Select Works,* and its inclusion is possibly due not to its merit, but to a wish to find a brief and thereby unobtrusive example of this part of his poetic corpus.

Dennis works several topics without special distinction. "To a Young Gentleman, Who Was Blam'd for Marrying Young" offers several horrible couplets, such as "Tell those who blame thee that till Thirty they / The noon of Life, for Love's chief meal may stay" (*Miscellanies,* 85). The strongest couplet in "To Mr. *E. H.* Physician and Poet" seems distinctive only in its lukewarmness: "Rise by vast Science and judicious rage, / Like

him [Phoebus] t' enlighten and to warm our Age" (*Miscellanies,*
84)—its other lines muddle along with even less inspiration.
Somewhat more interesting are two poems on a lady's picture,
which argue without much creativity that "Heavn's work, before
the Painter's we prefer, / Since it design'd its Master-piece in
her" (*Miscellanies,* 90). The amorous ditty "To *Flavia* Who
Fear'd She Was Too Kind" (the best of this verse) seems a
pieced-together combination of Cavalier seductiveness, Whig
pleading against a tyrant's "arbitrary Power," sexual description
complete with "panting Breasts" and the old sex-death pun,
and Neoplatonic love. It simply does not exhibit the nimbleness
and wholeness of vision found in earlier love poetry like Thomas
Carew's.

Dennis must write such poetry only because he feels expected
to. His strengths of logic and carefully examined evidence never
appear, and strong feeling seems to have no place. He obviously
cannot feel his mind and soul involved.

Battle Poetry

Seeking material that would both provide him with a grand
subject and let him serve his country, Dennis naturally came
upon battle poetry. He wrote several pure military poems (another poem, *The Monument,* contains military lines within a
larger structure), including one on a naval and three on land
triumphs. Although marred often by awkwardness and verboseness, most of them share the strengths of vivid description, clear
structure, and patriotic animation stemming from great martial
victory.

"Upon Our Victory at Sea, and Burning the *French* Fleet at
La Hogue," first published in the June 1692 *Gentleman's Journal,*
describes in heroic couplets the one outstanding English naval
triumph since the disgrace at Beachy Head in 1691. Failing
to get the proper reinforcements (or in the poet's phrase, "of
treacherous Aid deceiv'd"), the French admiral Tourville attacked the combined English and Dutch fleet, losing fifteen ships
and seeing his survivors dispersed. The English rejoiced, for
France thereafter could launch no major fleet action, being reduced to privateering.

The poem unfolds neatly: "Immortal Fury" inspires the poet,

the fleets noisily join in battle, various kinds of ammunition explode, Admiral Russell receives praise, and quiet returns after the destruction of French ships. The proud French are evil, as seen in phrases like "*Gallick* Demon" and "impious Colony." At the end their ships are likened to once proud oaks with mangled limbs, which now frighten rather than shelter.

Dennis enjoys writing furiously noisy passages:

> Their Rage by Loss of Limbs is kindled more,
> And with their Guns like Hurricanes they roar:
> Like Hurricanes the knotted Oak they tear,
> Scourge the vex'd Ocean, and torment the Air;
> While Earth, Air, Sea, in wild Confusion hurl'd,
> With universal Wrack and Chaos threat the World.
>
> (*SW,* 1:3)

His enthusiasm can result in awkward couplets, such as "There a red Bullet from our Cannon blown, / Into a First-Rate's Powder-Room is thrown"(*SW,* 1:4). However, perhaps because this is the shortest of his battle poems, Dennis shows here the best modulation of the sound level and the least wordiness.

He indicates his own high opinion of the poem by giving it first place in *The Select Works* (which is not arranged chronologically). A century later Robert Southey seems also to regard "Upon Our Victory" highly, since it is the only poem by Dennis that he prints in *Specimens of the English Poets.*

The year before the great naval victory, the English army scored a land victory at the Battle of Aughrim, in which several thousand fleeing Irish Catholic rebels lost their lives. Unfortunately, Dennis's much-ridiculed poetic tribute to this martial success, "A Pindarick Ode on the King . . . Occasion'd by the Victory at *Aghrim,*" little enhances his reputation. Although the poem rocks with much of the "loud Cannon and tempestuous Drums" of the 1692 poem, its unsure structure and many distractingly awkward couplets do not help the poet convey a tone of national ecstasy. We should feel no surprise that readers in Coleridge's day were still smiling at such lines as "Nor *Alps* nor *Pyreneans* keep it [War] out, / Nor fortify'd Redoubt" (*SW,* 1:28, 24).[7]

The other two battle poems, both much better than the Au-

ghrim tribute yet not themselves outstanding as poetry, laud
the Duke of Marlborough's victories.[8] The first, *Britannia Triumphans: or The Empire Sav'd, and Europe Deliver'd* (1704), recounts
the thrilling Battle of Blenheim, which resulted in 15,000
Franco-Bavarian casualties, 13,000 captives, the capture of the
French general Tallard, and Bavaria's withdrawal from the War
of the Spanish Succession. Contemporary newspaper accounts
and sermons exulted in the "Glorious Victory" by the valorous
Duke, and the Queen proclaimed a day of thanksgiving. Dennis
is but one of many poets rushing their verses into print to celebrate the mood.

Britannia Triumphans opens with appeals for inspiration, notably from the God of Revenge and Queen Anne, "Great Champi-
oness of Liberty and Faith" (*SW*, 1:156). The poet then asks
Germania, Austria, and Britannia to sing praise. We finally see
Marlborough, wise, majestically calm, decisive. After an allied
success at Schellenbourgh, the two sides poise for battle, which
then rages until the enemy fall into the Danube. The poem
ends with a quiet address to Death as Britannia mourns the
late sons of the Duke and of the Queen.

Dennis leaves no doubts about his sympathies: the Gallic tyrant, aided by his Jacobite friends in England, opposes liberty
and virtue. Marlborough, Anne's wondrous chief and Dennis's
military hero, has devised a battle plan, "His Essay, an Heroick
Master-piece, / Whose Brightness dazles all Spectators Eyes,
/ Astonishes our Friends, confounds our Foes" (*SW*, 1:172).
The hyperbolically praised Duke leads his men through the
noise of "The Trumpet's Roar! The Thunder of the Drum!"
to drown the enemy's pride in the horror of "the Cries, the
Shrieks, the dying Groans, / The Grief, the Rage, the Fury
of their Fear, / And all the Horrors of their baleful Eyes"
(*SW*, 1:199, 212–13).

Dennis is really too serious. He wishes so much to praise
Marlborough and Anne that he piles line upon line to produce
some fustian and much verboseness. Thus his 1,381 lines make
few solid points. He does not develop the skillful character
analysis or directness of Addison's 470-line *The Campaign,* written also to celebrate Blenheim. However, both poets received
tangible returns from the grateful Duke, Dennis getting a hundred pounds and the post of royal waiter in the London Custom-
House, Addison becoming undersecretary of state.

Dennis returns to Marlborough in *The Battle of Ramillia: or, The Power of Union* (1706), occasioned by a victory that resulted in 15,000 French deaths. He calls attention in both the dedication and the preface to his boldness in devising his Miltonesque tribute as "something of the Epick Kind" (*CW*, 1:394). Such boldness, however, does not here produce a satisfying poem.

The blank-verse lines divide into five books. In book 1, as the Confederate troops gather, Satan enviously recounts for his troops Marlborough's success at Blenheim and praises Louis XIV, "the second Hope of Hell, / The Man, the Monarch after my own Heart" (*SW*, 1:241); Discord pushes the spirits to defeat Anne and the Duke. Discord and Night in book 2 rekindle Louis's ambition by reminding him of Blenheim, "Blast to my Hopes of Universal Sway" (*SW*, 1:271). In book 3 the French leader Villeroy hears of the Confederate troops from Discord, who retells Marlborough's astounding deeds at Blenheim. An angel tells Marlborough in book 4 of his impending victory and his future joy in Heaven. Book 5 describes the Battle of Ramillies and the predicted Confederate victory.

Many elements of *The Battle of Ramillia* remind us too much of the Blenheim poem. Dennis ends up saying the same things about Marlborough and the satanic Louis. Strangely, we hear a great deal more about Blenheim than about Ramillies.

Two major differences between the two poems, length and epic machinery, support Cibber's judgment of the poem as "a cold unspirited performance; it has neither fire, nor elevation. . . ."[9] Dennis seems unable to handle the scope of 2,040 lines, writing the most repetitive and verbose passages of his career. The great reliance on heavenly and infernal spirits leads also to tedious pages heavy on abstractions and very light on concrete detail; after four books of anticipation, we see almost nothing of the Battle of Ramillies, since Dennis by now has stated all his abstract positions. Pope seems right in lampooning Dennis's machinery in *The Critical Specimen.*

Elegiac Political Verse

The Court of Death.   Poets striving for any kind of respectability during the late seventeenth century published lines on recently deceased figures of national importance. Thus hundreds of elegies inundated the bookstalls following Queen Mary's death of smallpox on 28 December 1694. The nation deeply lamented the passing of its virtuous queen. The universities, with their traditional flourish, published collections of tributes written in Latin, Greek, Hebrew, French, Modern English, Old English, Arabic, Persian, Turkish, Egyptian, Welsh, and other tongues. The many professional contributors included Cibber, Congreve, D'Urfey, Gould, Motteux, Prior, Steele, Tate, and Walsh. We even find a critical response to the poetic responses, *The Mourning Poets: or, An Account of the Poems on the Death of the Queen,* which satirizes the low overall quality of the poems:

> What bulky Heaps of doleful Rhyme I see!
> Sure all the World runs mad with Elegy;
> Lords, Ladies, Knights, Priests, Souldiers, Squires, Physicians,
> Beaux, Lawyers, Merchants, Prentices, Musicians,
> Play'rs, Footmen, Pedants, Scribes of all Conditions.[10]

Among the more original elegies is Dennis's *The Court of Death. A Pindarique Poem, Dedicated to the Memory of Her Most Sacred Majesty, Queen Mary.* "Bold in the design," this ode features a rare structure in a genre typified by unchanging structures. The poem contains three sections. In stanzas 1 through 4 the persona is visited at night by Pindar's Muse, who will show this poet the underworld Court of Death and help him "sing in wond'rous Rhyme / Of Things transcendently sublime" (*SW,* 1:36). In the grim "infernal Room," of stanzas 5 through 12, Death tries to motivate his ghastly crew by describing the keen frustration felt when William III, "Th'undaunted Hero," insolently braves and defeats death. Finally, Discord introduces a plan to destroy William by killing Mary; after some description of Mary's virtues, the poet awakens with the repeated chant, "Let this Good, this Great MARIA die" (*SW,* 1:59).

In the preface Dennis explains his wish to emulate Pindar's "vehemence, his impetuousness, and the magnificent sounds of his numbers; and . . . something dreadful, something which terribly shakes us, at the very same time it transports us" (*CW,* 1:43). He wants at the same time to imitate Milton, who shares much with Pindar. Conscious Miltonisms include the brightly shining Muse, the convocation of infernal spirits, and such phrases as "Adamantine Chains." And the style does indeed wax vehement. Death's followers roll, foam, roar, and bellow

> As when the Northern Tyrant of the Waves
> Upon the Polar Main in black *September* raves,
> The Billows, vex'd to madness, roar,
> And foaming scourge the gloomy dismal Shore.
> (*SW,* 1:48)

We can sense the author's ingenuity in finding his own way to mourn the queen. Most of her elegists simply catalog her virtues, particularly her goodness and beauty. Dennis instead creates the drama of the infernal conspiracy, an interesting feature of which is the implicit linking of "the raving *French*" with the lunatic spirits. Also, England's loss is both made poignant and rationalized when the queen becomes the only logical target of the impious conspirators because of her perfection: the woman Eve involved us in the Fall, but the woman Mary restores us to immortality.

Even if its lines do not have the resonance of great poetry, *The Court of Death* certainly shows improvement over Dennis's early witty verse. He develops his own effective structure, and he creates the passion he finds essential in greater poetry. Appropriately, *The Mourning Poets* singles out for highest praise the boldness and daring of Dennis's Pindaric flight.

The Monument. After William III died on 8 March 1702, elegies appeared very soon, although not in the great number penned upon Mary's death. Instead of his wife's beauty, William had a hooknosed face wrinkled by an asthmatic cough. Instead of her openness with the English people, he exhibited what seemed aloofness, due in large measure to his unfamiliarity with the English language and customs and his narrow education. Finally, his heartfelt devotion to frustrating Louis XIV kept the nation enmeshed in expensive, largely unpopular warfare.

But the king did stir in many thoughtful Englishmen strong gratitude for preserving the state during most uncertain times. His arrival from Holland prevented another civil war, and his single-minded concentration upon duty kept off the twin monsters of Gallic and papal dominion. We thus feel no surprise when an author who has just written a hundred pages quite objective in tone abruptly leaps into passionate commendation of this "Prince the best qualify'd for a Throne, being great without Pride, True to his Word, Wise in his Deliberations, Secret in his Counsels, Generous in his Attempts, Undaunted in Dangers, Valiant without Cruelty."[11] Nor should we feel surprise to find a Williamite mythology evolving to replace the old Stuart one.[12]

Since he could not fail to write something on his royal hero, three months after the king's death, Dennis published *The Monument: a Poem Sacred to the Immortal Memory of the Best and Greatest of Kings, William the Third, King of Great Britain, &c.* We find here the common overall elegiac structure of (1) lamentation, (2) praise, and (3) consolation.

(1) Distraught with sudden grief, the author asks Britannia, Batavia, Europa, Liberty, Religion, guardian angels, and the earth and heavens to mourn; the universe mourns because William blessed all. (2) Unlike satanic "vulgar" heroes (read "Louis"), the heroic William asserted God's governance of man's liberty; unlike Caesar, William conquered France for liberty, not pride; he won a glorious victory at Seneffe; he delivered England in the 1688 Revolution and Ireland at Boyne, but the populace showed no gratitude. (3) Since the king accepted death from God without complaint, we must not mourn but praise him; the author summarizes William's achievements, also briefly praising Queen Anne.

The most readable passages vividly describe the action at the Battle of Seneffe. Spurred on by "Death's Bugles in the dismal Chase of Blood," the soldiers find themselves in a cacophony of fire, cornets, drums, fiery heavens, outcries, volleys, and cannonades. The fighting makes "one ghastful Charnel of the Field" until the English "Storm of Iron Hail" finally ends the noise (*SW,* 1:118–22). Dennis here writes with crispness, verve, and dramatic pacing.

The poet's main end is to praise the king. This he does in part by offering William's enemies as foils. Louis, for instance, is viewed as a prowling wolf, a lawless ocean, a bestial rapist, "the grand Destroyer." Both Louis the satanic plotter (as in *The Court of Death*) and those Jacobite "Sons of Darkness" plotting the king's assassination stealthily form their damnable designs in a secrecy unlike William's openness in public actions.

In his lines straightforwardly praising William's virtues, Dennis's enthusiasm for his subject creates a problem of credibility. We have no trouble assenting to the king's ability to inspire his troops, since Dennis focuses on the battle that historically best demonstrates that ability. Nor do such lines as "O Greatness, to be found on Earth no more!" prove hard to accept, since they patently belong in the elegiac tradition (*SW*, 1:111). However, the author too readily assumes an identification of the king with God for us fully to accept the characterization. The opening stanza laments, "The Good, the Great, the Godlike WILLIAM's dead!" (*SW*, 1:87)—a line identical in phrasing to one on Mary except for the insertion of "Godlike." Like Ulamar in *Liberty Asserted*, William is "Like th' Offspring of the Gods, a Hero born" (*SW*, 1:103); but Ulamar is a totally fictional character. Still, Dennis could make such comparisons work poetically, did he not go a step beyond letting William act simply like God to make him God. We hear that William's "wondrous Zeal united Earth and Heav'n" and he sympathized even with his foes (this contradicts other lines in the poem) because he knew that all are "From one Divine Original deriv'd" (*SW*, 1:91–92). Dennis's hero-worship has created a William impossible to believe in.

The quality of Dennis's poetic style fails to match his optimism about his performance. He says in the dedication, "I have less Mistrust of it than of any thing I have done in Poetry. Besides, the Design and the Immortal Subject may supply in some measure the Weakness of my Performance" (*SW*, 1:86). *The Monument* demonstrates, however, that if the technical control proves too weak, even the best overall designer will write only lackluster poetry. In the preface Dennis cites Milton and others to prove that blank verse lets the poet exactly phrase the intended thought, but in his hands it leads also to lack of control. This we see particularly in the overexpansiveness of descriptive passages and the repetition of numerous phrases. We might also note one of the worst lines in battle poetry, where Dennis writes alliteratively of Fortune: "She to new Slaughter lash'd on limping Fate" (*SW*, 1:111).

We miss the compression and subtle rhythms of John Hughes's elegy on William, *The House of Nassau*. *The Monument* is a literary monument to Dennis's zeal, but it is not outstanding poetry.

Anne and George. Upon the 1 August 1714 death of Queen Anne, the last Stuart monarch, the crown passed to George of Hanover. A number of poems appeared to observe simultaneously the death and the accession. Many of these works mourn and praise Anne, introducing George only at the end as a consolatory motif. For instance, Edward Young devotes three-quarters of "On the Late Queen's Death, and His Majesty's Accession to the Throne" to Anne and the concluding one-quarter to George.

Dennis's *A Poem upon the Death of Her Late Sacred Majesty Queen Anne, and the Most Happy and Most Auspicious Accession of his Sacred Majesty King George* inverts this common structure to touch but lightly on Anne and say much about the new king. His poem divides into three parts: (1) the narrator summons Urania to help him picture Britain's woe and fear upon Anne's death; (2) all Britons, united in politics and religion and including William as commander of "the triumphant Slain," proclaim the arrival of George, who will rule by "Reason's Law"; (3) future benefits of union under George will include victory over foreign tyrants, the sending of British ships over the world, rich citizens' helping the poor, more commerce and agriculture, "Virtue under Liberty" (embracing the disappearance of idleness, luxury, and all passions but love), strengthened religion and fidelity to the nation, and victory for true writers.

Only stanza 1, less than 10 percent of the poem, refers to Anne. Even in this stanza, the discussion is generalized. The only specified accomplishment, the land victories against France, belongs in fact to Dennis's martial hero, Marlborough, not the queen. The woman is fast forgotten in the next stanza, where we find "*Britannia* passing in an Hour / From Fear to Hope, to Joy, to Extasy" (*SW,* 1:332). We feel no surprise, therefore, that in *The Select Works* Dennis has appropriately changed the title to "On the Accession of King George to the British Throne."

Dennis's slighting Anne indicates aversion to the late queen. Her Tory and High Church sympathies led her to create a Tory majority in the House of Lords and to support Henry Sacheverell, one of Dennis's bitter foes. She publicly exhibited jealousy toward George. And at the end her bewilderment about what to do made her a pathetic woman perhaps most memorable for her incredible record of twelve miscarriages and six short-lived children.[13] Dennis cannot find much to praise. In fact, most British citizens concurred; no royal monument was erected in her memory.

Although guaranteed by the 1701 Act of Settlement, the Hanoverian right to the throne was greatly complicated by the desperate actions of Tory leaders such as Bolingbroke shortly before Anne's death. Most of Dennis's poem reflects the author's joy that at last the Hanoverian Succession will have its chance to work. He foresees a moral change so great that "the true *Britannick* Tory, and Church Whig," and the dissenter will forget their distinctions within a new union. Actually, he is re-creating the Whigs' thrilling sense of victory, which they were to enjoy politically for many years.

In prophesying the benefits to be reaped, Dennis reaches back to the principles that he has supported in earlier works. Liberty over tyranny, the importance of commerce, responsibility to one's state, and the battle against "venal, vile, accursed Pens, / That with their Lyes intoxicate the Crowd" (*SW*, 1:353) are all here. We have before us almost a catalog of this writer's moral and political tenets.

In this, his last poem, Dennis writes a competent, interesting combination of halfhearted elegy and wholehearted anticipatory congratulation. True to his own beliefs, he looks forward to a dazzling era which he was never to enjoy.

Religious Verse

As seen in chapter 2, Dennis devoted much critical attention to the importance of religion in poetry. It may thus surprise us to discover that he wrote poetry wholly devoted to religion only three times, and all of these lines were originally incorporated into prose treatises.

We need pause but a moment over two fragmentary biblical paraphrases. In *The Advancement* Dennis had quoted the King James prose version of Psalm 18:6–15 as an instance of greatness in divine poetry. In *The Grounds,* obviously still impressed by the Psalmist, he offers his own poetic treatment of these same lines as well as of Habakkuk 3:3–15.

He aims in both translations to show how religion moves us to passion through such lines as

> The Mountains from their fix'd Foundations ran,
> And frighted from their inmost Caverns roar'd.
> From out his [the Lord's] Nostrils a tempestuous Cloud
> Of pitchy Smoke in spiry Volumes flew,
> And from his Mouth there ran a raging Flood
> Of torrent Fire, devouring as it ran.
>
> (*CW,* 1:367–68)

The technique of working a resounding vocabulary into unvaried, rolling blank-verse lines we have already seen in such writings as the battle poems. Unfortunately, these fragments come perilously closer to fustian than they should. They do, however, move with a strength that helps the essayist make his point; like him, we perhaps should not insist upon their being great lines.

Stronger as a poem in its own right is "Part of the *Te Deum* Paraphras'd, in Pindarick Verse." The original, a third-century Latin hymn by St. Ambrose beginning "Te Deum laudamus" ("We praise thee, O God"), comprises three chants. The first notes all those who praise God; the second describes Christ's deeds for man; the third prays for the Lord's blessing and mercy.

In his six-stanza version Dennis works on only the first chant, expanding upon the idea of how much in the universe praises God. The persona first bids all raise their voices to praise the eternal King, "permanent and fix'd, / Uncreated and unmix'd." In following stanzas we learn how earth's nonhuman creatures, man, and heavenly spirits "To sing Thee, Great Creator, all conspire, / All Ranks divinely touch the living Lyre" (*SW,* 1:11, 16). We at last find all together, worshiping the Lord of the immense universe.

The most noticeable weakness of the poem is verbose passages. Dennis tries to achieve a sense of spaciousness, expansion, and greatness by packing many lines with repetitions of phrasing or idea. For example, to suggest how creatures from absolutely every area of the physical world laud their Creator, he writes:

> Creatures, to whom great Mother Earth,
> Fermented by thy Flame, gave Birth;

All that on *Lybian* Mountains roar,
Or flounder on the *Indian* Shore;
All that in airy Caravans on high,
Intelligent of Seasons fly,
Thro the vast Desarts of th' Aerial Sky:
All to their Maker Adoration pay.

(*SW,* 1:12)

In terms of pure stylistics, we have here throwaway lines; however, even with their deficiencies of poetic style, the lines most surely convey Dennis's serious intent. We cannot fail to grasp his poetic logic, which derives from his philosophy of the highest poetry: if the world reflects the divine greatness, and the poet lives in the world, the greatest poetry will bring together those images, rhythms, and sounds found in the world that most tellingly suggest greatness. We may not find in the verses Milton's genius, but we can certainly feel the honest struggle of a minor poet to re-create his awe before the immensity of God's universe.

The *Te Deum* paraphrase enjoyed a moderately good reputation. The several editions of *A Collection of Divine Hymns and Poems upon Several Occasions,* first published in 1709, reprint the poem along with verses by the Earl of Roscommon, Dryden, and others. On 25 September 1724 the *Plain Dealer* glowingly congratulates the author for having "oblig'd the World, so nobly, in his *Paraphrase on Te Deum,* with Verse, and Sentiments, sublimely suited to the *Vastness* of the Occasion. . . . This is Poetry, that defies Censure, and is rais'd, even above Praise: for it is scarce possible to say so much of it, as it truly deserves." Some of Dennis's biographers temper their enthusiasm but remain positive in their overall verdict. Cibber finds the poem to confirm "that Mr. Dennis wrote with more elegance in Pindaric odes, than in blank verse," while Kippis feels that the paraphrase "is of superiour merit, though not entitled to any very high degree of praise."[14]

Dennis himself felt the highest regard for the poem. He first prints the entire paraphrase in *The Advancement,* where it helps prove the superiority of Christian to pagan poetry. In *The Grounds* he reproduces the final sixteen lines to show how the immensity of the universe can produce admiration. Still later, in a letter to the *Spectator,* he again quotes these sixteen lines

to prove that in *Tatler* 119 Steele has plagiarized ideas found
only in the paraphrase (unfortunately, an empty complaint, since
the ideas are almost commonplaces). Dennis also argues in this
letter that the translation is one of his strongest poems. However,
he did not in his later years attempt religious poetry. The power
of such late religious prose writings as his translations of Thomas
Burnet (1728 and 1730) indicates that for Dennis prose is a
more natural medium.

The Reverse

Dennis's most interesting poem, *The Reverse: or, The Tables
Turn'd* (1700), first ascribed to him in 1920, attacks John Tutchin's *The Foreigners* (1700). In many ways the Whig pamphleteer
Tutchin would seem a bedfellow to Dennis. He, too, pleaded
for naval reform, wrote anticlerical books, and proclaimed himself an asserter of English literties, and he died at the hands
of a pro-Sacheverell mob. Dennis, however, does not like Tutchin's discerning scandal where no evidence of wrongdoing exists.
As we learn in "The Author to the Reader," he views Tutchin
as a malcontent, a dull malignant, a blockhead.

Nor can Dennis accept the central point of *The Foreigners.*
Evincing marked xenophobia, Tutchin attributes England's troubles to the pernicious influence of foreign-born politicians. These
foreigners receive English titles, estates, wealth, and military
commands as they set aside native liberties and real Englishmen
become lackeys. Deep hatred seethes through lines describing
the Netherlands, homeland of William III and his closest advis-
ers:

> Its Natives void of Honesty and Grace,
> A Boorish, rude, and an inhumane Race;
> From Nature's Excrement their Life is drawn,
> Are born in Bogs, and nourish'd up from Spawn.[15]

Tutchin also presses the Republican claims for the people's right
to elect their king or to choose no king.

Dennis answers "Paragraph by Paragraph," printing his and
Tutchin's verses on alternating facing pages, so that we can
see "The Tables Turn'd." He argues that the foreign-born men

assailed by Tutchin have actually strengthened England. Before William's accession "Impious *Israelites* were *Israel*'s Foes" (*Reverse,* l. 6); as in Tutchin, "Israel" is England. Native moral corruption has long enervated the nation and shows in the influence of self-serving native politicians such as Sir Edward Seymour and in the "canker'd Malice" of Tutchin, vividly described as "a Senseless, starving Scribler" (*Reverse,* l. 83). The greatest threat is posed by Republicans like the insolent "High-Priest" Gilbert Burnet.

Like most effective controversialists, Dennis uses both emotional appeals and logic. We see the former in an attack on Tutchin: "Oh may the Calves-head Rioters, our Foes, / Still use *his* Rhimes, *his* lamentable Prose" (*Reverse,* ll. 97–98). Dennis is referring to the horrible blasphemies of the possibly mythical Calves' Head Club. According to Ned Ward, this group comprised extreme Republicans who annually derided monarchical rule by wickedly celebrating the assassination of Charles I. Their supposed ritual contained incidents disgusting to all good citizens: ". . . the Anniversary *Anthem,* as they impiously call'd it, was sung, and a Calves-Skull fill'd with Wine or other Liquor, and then a Brimmer went about to the Pious Memory of those worthy Patriouts that had kill'd the Tyrant, and deliver'd their Country from his Arbitrary Sway."[16] Such implications give Tutchin's arguments a tone of wildness and demonic conspiracy.

Dennis's logic shows best in his turning the thoughts in each of Tutchin's stanzas to the reverse thought. For example, across the page from his opponent's hateful description of the Netherlands Dennis places his most violent attack on Republicanism. Similarly, Tutchin's "If we a Foreign Slave may use in War, / Yet why in Council should that Slave appear?" turns into a strong complaint that England is shamefully disgracing her martial saviors by ostracizing them.[17] This method is carried out in every stanza, often with imagination, until Tutchin simply has no chance.

Although published only eighteen days after *The Foreigners,* Dennis's poem effectively counters Tutchin. It does not possess the imaginative power of Defoe's answer, *The True-Born Englishman;* but it certainly has more subtlety and originality than other responses, such as the anonymously published *The Natives*

(1700). Yet, as well as Dennis and Defoe wrote, they did not destroy their opponent, for next year he is still asking, "Must *Foreign* Councils manage our Intrigues, / And make our *Treaties,* and confirm our *Leagues?*"[18]

The high quality of *The Reverse* does not result from Dennis's applying his critical theories about poetry. Treatises like *The Advancement* and *The Grounds* describe the ends of the highest poetry, which the lines against Tutchin clearly are not intended to achieve. The dully methodical and unimaginative "Of Prosody," first printed in the second edition of James Greenwood's *An Essay towards a Practical English Grammar* (1722), puts forward some mechanical rules for composing but gives no hint that its author could write poetry that makes us either think or feel. Rather, Dennis in *The Reverse* uses the couplet wit learned from Butler and Dryden and the brisk verbal aggressiveness already developing in his own controversial prose.

Chapter Six

Noncritical Prose

We cannot possibly gauge Dennis's thought without knowing his pamphlets on nonliterary topics. It is no accident that his literary criticism and his creative literature so often stress morality, taste, patriotism, and religious sensibility. The noncritical pamphlets indicate that throughout his maturity he was grappling directly with such ideas. Examining his society from the viewpoint of a Neoplatonist (as noted in the earlier discussion of *The Grounds*), he finds abundant evidence of our fall from perfection.

In one handful of writings, he accuses his fellow citizens of a corruption of spirit and taste debasing all elements of society. In another group he outlines a program of moral and administrative reform within the country's naval forces. Finally, he also writes pamphlets angrily denouncing contemporary religious bigots and sedately anticipating the afterlife.

Public Morality

An Essay on the Opera's. Dennis's first pamphlet devoted entirely to moral corruption attacks Italian opera. The English audience had long accepted operatic elements on the stage. Tragedies and comedies offered many songs and dances—witness, for instance, Ophelia's song fragments in act 4 of *Hamlet* and the dancing at the end of *A Midsummer Night's Dream.* Heroic plays established the dramatic usefulness of spectacular scenic effects. And the masque combined music, dialogue, dance, and often elaborate scenery. Nonetheless, the audience before 1700 felt unsure about dramas in which the music outweighed the words. In the English opera, such as those composed by Purcell, we have a "spoken play with interpolated all-sung masques"; the audience can still hear spoken dialogue.[1]

However, the staging of Thomas Clayton's 1705 *Arsinoe,*

Queen of Cyprus (an all-sung opera in the Italian style), the exclusive devotion of the new Haymarket Theater to opera, and the sudden demand for Italian singers indicated that the public would now accept stage productions in which the words could be subordinated to the music, perhaps could not even be understood!

Critical response to such entertainment was heavily negative. Dryden ridiculed the Italian braying of "amorous asses," Johnson found the Italian opera "exotick and irrational entertainment," Pope saw the "Harlot form" seducing onlookers into nonsense, Gay parodied the form in *The Beggar's Opera,* and Addison, Swift, Downes, and many others added their condemnations. The most common objections concern undue foreign influence, a lessened respect for clarity and sense on the stage, and adverse effects upon spectators' character.

Dennis contributes one of the strongest and fullest statements of this misgiving in *An Essay on the Opera's after the Italian Manner, Which Are About To Be Establish'd on the English Stage: With Some Reflections on the Damage Which They May Bring to the Publick* (1706). As the title suggests, he intends not simply to throw a few accusatory darts but to elaborate a moral treatise for the good of his country. This he does in four steps: (1) In the preface he stresses the desperate importance of the problem, reviewing his main points about the advantages of dramatic presentations from *The Usefulness of the Stage* and indicting "that soft and effeminate Musick which abounds in the *Italian Opera"* (*CW,* 1:384). (2) The *Essay* proper begins with a patriotic warning that while England's military prove victorious, English arts may fall to this "Invasion of Foreign Luxury," an art not subservient to reason. (3) Dennis proceeds to argue that establishing Italian opera will drive out poetry, because audiences, disinclined to think or use common sense, will praise and reward only plays filled with empty song and dance; playwrights will then give the public exactly what it wants. (4) He concludes by predicting an eclipse of the national reputation and interest as "soft and delicious Musick" destroys public virtue and spirit, the people move closer toward slavery, and other nations scorn England.

Dennis seems wholly sincere in describing the moral effect of Italian opera. His tone is quite unlike that of Charles Gildon, who in 1710 assails "the Absurdities of *Opera's;* I think the Degeneracy of the Age is but too apparent, in the setting up and encouraging so paltry a Diversion, that has nothing in it either manly or noble."[2] Gildon is but one of several critics who blandly stay with Dennis's generalizations, not trying to show why such a case is "too apparent." Dennis, in contrast, wrestles hard with the problem.

He cannot unthinkingly condemn all theatrical music, since "there is no Man living who is more convinc'd than my self of the Power of Harmony, or more penetrated by the Charms of Musick. I know very well that Musick makes a considerable Part both of Eloquence and of Poetry" (*CW,* 1:385). In his own dramas, particularly *Rinaldo and Armida,* music and some rather spectacular stage effects help him establish themes and moods. He feels obliged, then, to prove the unacceptability of one kind of theatrical music.

We see Dennis's individuality of argument most clearly in his psychological logic. He fears that when music no longer serves reason but grows "independent, as it does in our late Operas, it becomes a mere sensual Delight, utterly incapable of informing the Understanding, or reforming the Will; and for that very reason utterly unfit to be made a publick Diversion; and then the more charming it grows, it becomes the more pernicious. Since when it is once habitual, it must so far debauch the Minds of Men, as to make them incapable of those reasonable Diversions, which have got the just Possession of the Stage" (*CW,* 1:385–86). The subsequent causal analysis follows directly from such theorizing, which combines Dennis's conceptions of reason, passion, and the place of art in social reform.

The psychosocial theory of climatic influence figures prominently. For example, because modern Italians have the same climate as the ancient Romans, we would expect the two peoples to act alike; that they do not (Dennis always admires the true Roman virtue of old) he traces to the only variable, modern Italian luxury, the most flagrant being opera. In a more interesting application of the climatic theory, Dennis claims that England has neither the language (English is too masculine) nor the climate proper to opera. Most other Christian nations are more "qualify'd to surpass us in Operas, since they are almost all situated under a serener Sky. . . . As all Kingdoms that are in different Latitudes, have Plants with very different Properties, so have they Natives with very different Talents" (*CW,* 1:392). This reasoning may seem preposterous today, but to many contemporaries, including Addison and Congreve, such an application of the climatic theory would make good sense. Above all, it shows Dennis working very hard to establish basic explanations.

Dennis relies also on the test of experience. His knowledge of Greek, Roman, and English history, albeit selective in its detail, lets him predict the consequence of unceasing approval of Italian opera, and his condemnation of the public clamor for nonsensical entertainments takes on deep pessimism in large measure because he has personally witnessed the silliness. His letters (as in *OL,* 1:65) reveal his familiarity with such popular novelties as masquerades, Italian farce, French tumblers, puppets, clowns, and strongmen. Dennis's tone conveys a thinking man's complete disdain for performers like the acrobat at Drury Lane who can "vault on the manag'd Horse, where he lyes with his Body extended on one Hand in which posture he drinks several Glasses of Wine with the other, and from that throws himself a Sommerset over the Horses' Head, to Admiration."[3]

Kippis writes, "His violent declamation against operas and music is not sufficiently justified by reason and experience. Such declamation was partly the fashion of the most eminent writers of the time."[4] But Dennis most surely wants to express something beyond merely fashionable ideas; in fact, we sense individually felt desperation. Furthermore, he is writing true to experience as he knows and interprets it. Finally, even if we cannot accept his reasoning, he takes it seriously here and follows it in other writings.

Modern readers who find Dennis's arguments unacceptable because of quaintness or vehemence should put themselves back three hundred years and into the mind of this writer. He feels frustration that many worthwhile plays, his own included, do not receive proper attention, while an explosively popular new artistic medium leads a host of novelties onto a stage that has little room for the kind of play that he knows. His frustration increases with his not understanding the ground rules for evaluating the new form and feeling certain that its adherents likewise cannot understand why they support it. We must credit Dennis with the honesty to attempt a rational, consistent explanation of his deeply felt, perhaps nearly instinctive aversion. We might even feel, as Cibber does, an irresistible force in this essay; we certainly find a highly individual treatment of a significant issue.

An Essay upon Publick Spirit. Italian opera was for Dennis only one sign of national corruption. He attacks the problem in greater breadth in *An Essay upon Publick Spirit; Being a Satyr in Prose upon the Manners and Luxury of the Times, the Chief Sources of Our Present Parties and Divisions* (1711). After a preface calling for a luxury tax and laws against gaming and dueling, he develops in the two-chapter *Essay* itself the argument that England must restore its original public spirit. In chapter 1 he defines public spirit as "the ardent Love of one's Country, affecting us with a zealous Concern for its Honour and Interest, and inspiring us with Resolution and Courage to promote its Service and Glory" (*SW*, 1:407). He proceeds with examples from Rome, Greece, England, and France to argue that citizens will feel this spirit only if they love the manners peculiar to their own nation.

In chapter 2 he finds that modern Englishmen have lost their ancestors' stolid manners without replacing them with suitable conduct of their own, introducing ruinous foreign manners and luxuries. The healthy England of Henry VII exhibited religious sincerity, frugality, temperance, dignity, moderation of passions, liberality, noble activity for the national good and glory, absence of factions, and contempt for luxurious arts and foreign customs. But public spirit today has disappeared within a chaotic nightmare of religious anarchy, individual pride and luxury, such destructive foreign luxuries as French wine and Italian opera, gaming, indebtedness, and slander.

By far the most interesting passages come in chapter 2, as Dennis translates his distress into vituperation against foreign luxury. For instance, he loathes debauching wines and French dishes with "their high aromatick Sauces, those fierce Incendiaries of the Blood and Spirits," both of which produce distempers and "an Infinity of irregular Desires, unlawful Amours, Intrigues, and Vapours, and Whimsies, and all the numerous melancholy Croud of deep hysterical Symptoms." Italian opera fares no better, being labeled "the Burlesque of Catterwawling,

where Love and Battel are wag'd together with a perpetual
Squawling (*SW,* 1:423, 434). Verbal blows accumulate into a
massive, many-fronted assault upon what Dennis is certain has
produced the general moral collapse he sees everywhere. That
is, strongly assailing one example after another rhetorically
pushes us to understand and accept his notion of the overall
cause.

The *Essay,* however, does not prove wholly satisfactory. We
do not find the depth of psychological explanation that gives
the *Essay on the Opera's* much of its distinction. Taking here
an easier route, Dennis gives us his conclusions about the pernicious effects of various luxuries without trying to analyze how
those effects come about. Many pages of the *Essay* are also no
more than repetition of attitudes found in the opera pamphlet.
Thus, as accurately as the *Essay* reflects Dennis's moral distress
at the ruinous effect of foreign customs, if we already know
the earlier work, we find here little new of any real substance.

Julius Caesar Acquitted.   On 2 and 9 December 1721,
Thomas Gordon published in the *London Journal* two letters
that appalled Dennis. Gordon, writing as "Cato," argues that
Brutus acted the hero in assassinating Julius Caesar, "a publick
Oppressor, Scourge, Usurper, Executioner, and Plunderer" who
acted "like a Barbarous Conqueror and an Alien." Gordon
shares his judgment of Caesar with the great majority of contemporary authors of all political leanings, who seized upon the
Roman dictator as a convenient symbol of tyranny.[5] Thus many
Whigs equate James II with Caesar (or Augustus), William with
Brutus, the Pretender with a new Augustus. Many Tories, meanwhile, equate the Roman tyrant with William or one of the
Hanoverian Georges (George I was christened George Augustus). Gordon's Republican sympathies give these *Cato's Letters*
an unmistakable meaning: Republicanism is the best form of
government, but England ("Rome") has so degenerated that
the monstrous tyrant George is temporarily necessary.

Dennis responded to these "flaming and outrageous Things"
in *Julius Caesar Acquitted, and His Murderers Condemn'd. In a Letter
to a Friend. Shewing, That It Was Not Caesar Who Destroy'd the
Roman Liberties, but the Corruptions of the Romans Themselves. . . .
To Which Is Added, a Second Letter, Shewing, That If Ever the Liberties
of Great Britain Are Lost, They Will Be Lost No Other Way than*

by the Corruptions of the People of Great Britain Themselves (1722). In his preface Dennis warns of "ill-designing Men" abusing the widespread anti-Caesar prejudice to introduce Roman Catholic rule or a republic. His first letter debates the legality of all assassinations and promotes the basely murdered Caesar's nobility. With the second letter Dennis returns to his oft-stated tenet that a free people's liberty depends basically upon their uncorrupted manners and consequent public spirit.

The first letter contains Dennis's freshest and strongest material. He writes, "In short, if Assassinations are allow'd to be lawful even upon the most provoking Motives, and consequently the Assassinators are allow'd to be Judges of the Lawfulness of what they undertake, why then no Prince or supream Magistrate . . . who has disoblig'd any number of Men . . . can be safe or secure. For the Assassinators being guided by Passion, and not by Reason, will under the cloak of specious Pretences carry on the most villainous Designs."[6] His rigorous logic underscores a difficulty that has always plagued crimes of conscience. We also find here his fear of chaos whenever passion displaces reason. The character sketch of Caesar recalls Dennis's pages in the earlier *Essay on the Genius and Learning of Shakespear,* where he judges the Roman leader a great man who seized power because Rome had lost its liberty and who meant to restore that liberty. Dennis now shows that "his vast Capacity and his matchless Valour made him the fittest to command; and his several Virtues, his Humanity, his Bounty, and his unequal'd Clemency, made him the best and most desirable Master" (*Julius Caesar Acquitted,* 22). This Caesar manifests the true Roman virtue of which Dennis approves in *The Invader of His Country,* published only two years earlier.

The strongest parts of the second letter do little more than repeat Dennis's argument about the disastrous effect of moral corruption upon public spirit from *An Essay on the Opera's* and *An Essay upon Publick Spirit.* More original but also far more questionable is his naive contention that the king and his ministers will never try to subvert English liberties because they fear what would happen to them.

Julius Caesar Acquitted does not succeed as a major pamphlet, mainly because of its repetitiveness. However, Dennis pursues his logical proofs, uses sources (especially Sallust and Plutarch) with care, and, once more true to character, adheres to a defiantly independent thesis. Most importantly, he gets behind the political rhetoric of the Caesar analogy pressed by Gordon and many others to emphasize what he feels to be the more important moral conflicts usually overlooked in using such rhetoric. For Dennis, debating Caesar's character does not take us far enough; we must ascertain a leader's place within the moral history of his nation.

Vice and Luxury Publick Mischiefs.   In the following year Bernard Mandeville published a work that horrified Dennis into his final defense of morality. Mandeville had in 1705 published *The Grumbling Hive,* a verse fable arguing that in flourishing states we inevitably find vice. The 1714 *The Fable of the Bees* had reprinted the poem and supplied prose "Remarks" showing how vices like pride and luxury produce national greatness. The 1723 edition now expanded the "Remarks" and added two essays, one of them "An Essay on Charity and Charity-Schools."[7]

Mandeville outraged many with the bold idea of his paradoxical subtitle, "Private Vices, Publick Benefits," which means that the selfish passions condemned by moralists can, if carefully managed, benefit the whole society. He shocked readers with his seemingly brutal approach and style: "The Chief Thing . . . which Lawgivers and other wise Men, that have laboured for the Establishment of Society, have endeavour'd, has been to make the People they were to govern, believe, that it was more beneficial for every Body to conquer than indulge his Appetites, and much better to mind the Publick than what seem'd his private Interest."[8]

If we get a feel for his paradoxical, complexly ironic thought, we find Mandeville expressing moral indignation with a disturbing frankness. Rather than soften the impact of our true motives, he exposes them in all their rawness. He is trying to express what he sees as moral truth in a way that will shock us into recognition.

Dennis responds in *Vice and Luxury Publick Mischiefs: or, Remarks on a Book Intituled, The Fable of the Bees,* his verbal play on Mandeville's subtitle indicating disbelief in Mandeville's moral soundness. "Writ in the Cause of the Christian Religion, of the Moral Virtue of Mankind, and of the Constitution and

Liberties of *Great Britain,"* the book attacks the spokesman for
all the corrupters assailed in the earlier moral treatises. "For,
to shew the utmost Profligacy of the Times which we live in,"
he charges, "Vice and Luxury have found a Champion and a
Defender, which they never did before."[9] The attack consists
of five sections: the dedication, the three-chapter *Remarks* themselves, and four letters (three addressed to Blackmore) with
"A Short Discourse."

The dedication responds to Mandeville's accusation that charity schools, established in several hundred parishes to improve
lower-class children, actually harm society and these children
themselves because they come to scorn their proper lot of "hard
and dirty Work." Dennis, finding Mandeville to lack charity,
argues from a different viewpoint: these children, uneducated,
would neither know true Christian doctrine nor elect representa-
tives wisely.

In the *Remarks* proper Dennis uses logic, authority, and examples to make three points: (1) vices and luxury do not benefit
but undermine public liberty, as shown, for instance, by the
current national debt; (2) moral virtue originates in natural law,
not politicians' contrivances; (3) luxury harms the state, "since
it weakens Mens Bodies, stupifies their Minds, consumes their
Substance, and wastes their Time, and keeps even those in a
State of Indolence and Inactivity, who are by Nature Diligent
and Industrious" (*Vice and Luxury,* 74–75). The final section
supports the established Christian religion; the "Short Discourse" is a reprint of part of *Advancement,* which Dennis obviously finds still valid.

Mandeville insists in *A Letter to Dion,* "Tho' I have shewn
the Way to Worldly Greatness, I have, without Hesitation, pre-
ferr'd the Road that leads to Virtue. . . . unless I was a Fool,
or a Madman, I could have no Design [in *The Fable*] to encour-
age or promote the Vices of the Age."[10] However, most readers,
including Dennis ("A noted Critick"), have misread *The Fables*
to find him encouraging vice. What Dennis fails to see, because
he does not read paradox well and puts morality uppermost,
is that he insists on a moral "should be" while Mandeville insists
on a description of what actually "is." Yet, we must respect
Dennis for maintaining his principles, perhaps not as systematically as George Bluet or as passionately as William Law in their

answers to Mandeville, but certainly with energy and careful, clearminded scholarship.

The Naval Pamphlets

The Seamens Case and *An Essay on the Navy.*   Among Dennis's more substantial contributions to contemporary social thought must be counted his first naval pamphlets, on abuses against sailors in the English navy.[11] On 16 January 1699/1700, "A Petition of *John Dennis*, on the behalf of several Thousand Seamen, was presented to the House" of Commons.[12] Probably in 1700 (known copies lack dated title-pages) this petition was published along with "The Address presented to the Lords of the Admiralty in Feb. 1698/9," all under the petition title *The Seamens Case with Respect to Their Service in the Navy, Wherein Divers Hardships Which They Undergo Are Truly Stated, and Humbly Presented to His Majesty and Both Houses of Parliament.*

The address, printed on one crowded page, asks that unpaid seamen be paid their wages. Specifically, Dennis asks that the queries and runs (explained below) be removed from the sailors' names. The petition expands the complaint to twelve grievances: (1) the unfair marking of queries against sick men, (2) the unfair marking of runs, (3) and (7) nonpayment of wages to agents empowered to collect them, (4) nonpayment of wages to seamen who are "turned over" (ordered to change ships), (5) turning men over too often, (6) demoting officers to decrease their wages, (8) low wages, (9) and (10) the difficulty of families' collecting monies due them upon sailors' deaths, (11) superior officers' vice and debauchery, (12) fraudulent wage requests, which weaken all seamen's claims.

By 1702 Dennis's thoughts had ripened fully into the form of a fifty-three-page book entitled *An Essay on the Navy, or England's Advantage and Safety, Prov'd Dependant on a Formidable and Well-Disciplined Navy; and the Encrease and Encouragement of Seaman.*[13] The *Essay* emphasizes (1) the importance of a strong English navy, with a documented analysis of the required number of ships and men (*Essay on the Navy,* 1–6); (2) the seamen's grievances making naval service unpopular, including unfair and violent treatment by captains, turning men over, intricate payment methods that long delay or deny wages, querying men, marking men as run, and impressment (*Essay on the Navy,* 6–33); (3) proposals to improve the 1696 act for registering seamen, perfect the wage ticket system, and increase the revenues of Greenwich Hospital (*Essay on the Navy,* 33–53).

Throughout these two pamphlets Dennis shows full awareness of major social and political currents. Numerous pamphleteers of the late seventeenth and early eighteenth centuries agreed with the Marquis of Halifax's assumption that "the first article of an Englishman's political creed must be, that he believeth in the sea."[14] Such a belief assumed a more urgent cast as the commercial and military competition with France, as well as competition with the merchant marine, created a desperate manpower shortage in the navy. Unfortunately, inaction on the part of the Admiralty and Parliament made it impossible to produce the needed men: England seemed on the edge of disaster.

The *Essay* catches the full spirit of the problem when we read that English honor and renown "must be maintained by the Strength, Valour and Prowess of our Forces by Sea, and that cannot be without a sufficient and well-disciplin'd Navy" (*Essay on the Navy,* 2). However, the recent near-success of Louis XIV—"that potent and politick Prince, who already seems to despise the whole Power of Europe" (*Essay on the Navy,* 3)—against the English grand fleet indicates something wrong at the heart of the English system. In analyzing this malady and its cure, Dennis goes well beyond other pamphleteers in his combination of command of detail, emotional appeal, and humanitarianism.

Despite the charges against naval officials, Dennis's familiarity with their needs assures us of his fairness. For example, the *Essay* contains charts and figures closely analyzing the 181 fighting ships of the fleet, their 10,000 cannon, and the 40,000 people needed to man them. The rigorousness of his computations is evident: "So that if 40000 Men be required . . . and two thirds of those, *viz.* 26666, are Officers, and Officers Servants, ordinary Seamen, Landmen, Gromets, and Boys, the other third, *viz.* 13334, able Seamen, besides those Officers, &c. are as many as were at any time employ'd in the Navy, during the late War" (*Essay on the Navy,* 5–6). Dennis's longstanding friendship with the Earl of Pembroke, the Lord High Admiral, to whom he dedicated the *Essay,* further confirms our view of the author as a man writing from firsthand appreciation of the navy's difficulties.

Beginning particularly with the 1688–97 war, the navy could not attract enough volunteers. Despite such advantages as the chance for promotion, disability pensions, prize money, and high wages compared to those paid laborers ashore, a naval career appealed to only a small proportion of workers, certainly not the 40,000 men desired. Most of the fleet were obtained by pressing unwilling people into service, a forerunner of modern military conscription.

Dennis argues not so much the illegality as "*the Inconveniences and Disadvantages of Impressing*" (*Essay on the Navy*, 30). Carefully showing recent statistics and his own computations, he notes such unnecessary expenses as rental for press vessels, press gangs' wages, provisions for impressed men not yet on ships, and losses among traders who rely upon watermen. Much like Defoe in the *Essay upon Projects* (1697), the *Review* for 13 January 1704/5, and a January 1704/5 letter to the House of Lords,[15] Dennis concentrates on hard financial detail to assail a practice that he abhors. But as if economic losses are not enough, he cites also "the frequent Riots, Tumults, and Quarrels, that happened as well amongst the Press-Gangs (in Cutting, Hewing, and Knocking down each other)" (*Essay on the Navy*, 31). This recruitment technique obviously little enhances the right naval discipline, just as it little reflects the social discipline Dennis finds so vital to the national well-being.

Far more pages focus on the inefficient and grossly unfair payment methods. Because of its acute cash shortage, the government could not pay all its sailors. Dozens of pamphleteers attack this long, deep-rooted failure. As Thomas Robe notes, "during our Wars with the *French* in our late Reigns, Complaints of this Kind were so loud, so miserable, and so numerous, that they pierc'd the Hearts of every *Englishman*, exepting [*sic*] such as were the principal Authors."[16] Unlike almost every other writer, Dennis piles example upon example of entire crews unpaid for several years and individuals whose wages are forever lost perhaps only because they were not aboard a ship on the day it was visited by an official paymaster. Such losses, he notes, seem particularly unjust when the man has been turned over.

Dennis pays special attention to the mechanisms underlying

the most flagrant abuses: the use of tickets and the Q's and R's. A ticket was no more than an IOU from the government. Because sailors and their families could not wait several months for the full monies to become available, they often had to sell their tickets to ticket-buyers at heavy discounts.[17] A "Q" ("Query") against a man's name in the paybook meant that he had been put ashore ill, while an "R" ("Run") signified desertion; in either case he could not receive wages. Bureaucratic chaos assured thousands of sailors that their Q's and R's would never be removed.

Reminding us of his earlier remarks in *The Seamens Case,* Dennis patiently refutes each possible defense of current payment methods. He again cites numerous examples, such as one John Searle, who was asked "*how, and by whom he was noted to be R. Which Query being impossible for him to answer, his R cou'd not be taken off*" (*Essay on the Navy,* 25)! Dennis never assaults those responsible for such illogic—he always labels his opponents "Gentlemen"—but his close detail clearly proves their fault.

Dennis always shows a humanitarian concern for the suffering. He fully agrees with earlier writers (several of whom he quotes) like Robert Crosfeild, who observes, "The poor Sailers that venture their Lives and Limbs . . . have been all along most inhumanly and barbarously treated, and they and their Families reduced to a miserable and deplorable State."[18] Dennis's pages run over with "oppressed," "suffer," "cruel"—all emotionally charged terms. Most examples vividly re-create suffering, especially when Dennis describes the curses and physical punishment inflicted upon seamen.[19] He recounts, for instance, how John Savage's captain "whipt and pickled him to that degree, that none believ'd he could live, leaving such Marks of his Kindness in his Back, that Men could bury their Fingers therein" (*Essay on the Navy,* 10).

In his proposals for reform, Dennis shows close familiarity with the 1696 Registry Act. One of its purposes was to recruit 30,000 seamen, but it raised only half that number. Dennis clear-sightedly offers several reasons for failure, such as "Cobblers, Barbers, Alehouse-keepers . . . grave Seniors" unfit for service joining for the money. The major problem, however, is that men are free to register or not. His solution: set up a national system by which each parish would register and keep track of a certain number of seamen. He carefully works out small details, including who does what and possible objections; he also ties in improvements in wage payment and ways to improve the Greenwich Hospital.

Dennis's proposals had little immediate impact. Throughout the next century writers still describe press gangs, late payment, flogging—all that Dennis pictures. In fact, conditions did not greatly improve until Victoria's reign. Dennis and dozens of other reformers had found an institutionalized wrong not soon to be eradicated.

In themselves, however, Dennis's two pamphlets are well done. John Ehrman finds *The Seamens Case* "the most persuasive" of the petitions against the Q's.[20] The changes in the registry suggested in the *Essay* are sensible enough to have been reproduced by other writers several years later.[21] Knowledge, compassion, and well constructed argument make the *Essay* Dennis's best work in his social pamphlets.

A Proposal for Putting a Speedy End to the War. Far less impressive is *A Proposal for Putting a Speedy End to the War, by Ruining the Commerce of the French and Spaniards, and Securing Our Own, without Any Additional Expence to the Nation* (1703). Dennis offers here an unfeasible solution to the thorny problem of French privateers during the War of the Spanish Succession.

After their naval defeat in the 1692 Battle of La Hogue, Jean Bart and other French seamen realized that they had to refocus their maritime strategy. As Admiral Herbert Richmond writes, "the war of fleets gave way to cruiser warfare directed against commerce, and commerce destruction, originally diversionary in its object, now assumed the form of a primary effort with decisive results in view."[22] The *guerre de course* had much to do with the decline in English merchant shipping from 340,000 tons in 1686 to 323,000 tons in 1702.[23]

The *Proposal* follows a classic argumentative proposal structure: (1) introduction of the intent, (2) specific procedure, (3) benefits, (4) answers to objections, (5) conclusion.

The opening pages carefully establish the importance of trade, the inability of present naval forces to stop French privateers, and the consequent need for "an additional Maritime Force, to secure our Commerce and ruin that of the Enemies" (*SW,*

1:384). England will provide two hundred medium-sized ships, as will the Dutch. Each nation will raise the yearly £500,000 expense by collecting import-export "Insurance-Money" from merchants, since they will reap the ultimate benefits. We also learn where ships will patrol, for example, "five between *Calais* and *Havre de Grace*" (*SW*, 1:388).

Overall advantages, Dennis argues, are twofold. First, since French privateers will be destroyed or chased off by the four hundred nimble ships, English trade will recover. Second, strategic placement of ships will ruin the enemies' commerce by cutting their trade routes.

To refute major objections, Dennis turns to moral argument and abstract logic. Merchants and the Dutch cannot possibly complain about financing the project, because "they shew themselves unreasonable to set an inconsiderable Overplus of sordid Gain in the Ballance against all this" (*SW*, 1:393). The French and Spanish privateers will not fight bravely, since they act solely out of self-interest, while under this plan the English and Dutch will "fight for their Country's Interest and their own" (*SW*, 1:400). Finally, the national debt will not be forced higher, for England will lose fewer ships, the government will not borrow further, and the war will end sooner.

If Parliament likes the idea, "I make no doubt but it will be follow'd," so that the English "remain a free Independent People" (*SW*, 1:405). As the dedication emotionally prays, Dennis also views his proposal as the salvation of the royal house: "while She [Queen Anne] with Mildness governs the Land, may your Highness with Terror controul the Main, and appear, to the Confusion of our Enemies, the dreadful Wonder of God in the Deep."[24]

Despite the sound structure, the sense of logic, and some originality of thought, the pamphlet fails. Dennis overlooks basic psychological reality when he argues that the merchants and the Dutch will pay £1,000,000 yearly just to avoid being judged unreasonable. Although he writes from "the Sense of the Duty that I owe my Country" (*SW*, 1:405), he shows naiveté in assuming that others will apply the same idea and make huge financial outlays. He also minimizes many political, economic, and legal complications involved in parliamentary decisions concerning trade and war.

Perhaps Dennis recognizes such inherent problems. For sure, the *Proposal* lacks the impassioned drive of the *Essay.* And although he again defended his *Proposal* in the preface to *Liberty Asserted* (1704) and a 1706 letter, eight years elapsed before he published another political pamphlet.

Christian Pamphlets

Attacks on religious bigotry. Strident religious controversy issued from the early eighteenth-century clash between Low and High Church viewpoints. Low Churchmen more likely supported toleration for dissenters and other Whiggish tendencies and placed relatively little emphasis on uniformity of belief, traditional rituals, or the priesthood. The 1689 Toleration Act signaled a new age for English Christians. Although not applicable to Roman Catholics or Unitarians, the act allowed many nonconformists their own houses of worship. Such a tendency gratified Low Churchmen, especially those Whigs looking toward full toleration for all sects. But it horrified High Church clergymen, who saw church and state being undermined.

One of the strongest and the best known of High Church spokesmen was Henry Sacheverell. Rising from a background of poverty and indifferent scholarship, he quickly gained power, becoming bursar of Magdalen College, Oxford, at thirty-five. In his sermons and pamphlets, he argued with violent language and appeals to popular prejudice that made him influential in church and secular politics. He was by 1710 so powerful that his impeachment by the Whigs for publishing *The Perils of False Brethren* "with a wicked, malicious and seditious intention to undermine and subvert her Majesty's government and the Protestant succession" resulted in explosions by Tory mobs and the downfall of the Whig ministry.[25]

Dennis felt impelled to answer an early Sacheverell work, *The Political Union.* This pamphlet supports a two-part proposition: "*That Religion is the Grand Support of Government*" and "*that the Peace, Happiness and Prosperity of the Secular and Civil Power, depends upon that of the Spiritual and Ecclesiastical.*" When the argument begins to focus on England, the logic fast becomes slippery: "But These Shuffling, Treacherous, *Latitudinarians,* ought to be Stigmatiz'd, and Treated Equally as Dangerous Enemies to the *Government,* as well as *Church:* For the *Royal Throne,* and the *Divine Altar,* seem so Inseparably Join'd and United in Each Others Interests, that the *One* can only be Maintain'd by the True Principles and Establishment of the *Other* . . . [;] where the *Ecclesiastical Body* is Infested with the One, the *Body Politick,* is seldom found Free from the Other Plague.'' Gross prejudice erupts as Sacheverell condemns the Toleration Act as a way to admit unto the church vipers, heterogeneous foreigners, and renegades. His inflammatory rhetoric would suit the most rabid mob: "We must Watch against These Crafty, Faithless, and Insidious Persons, who can *Creep* to Our Altars, and Partake of Our Sacraments, that They may be *Qualify'd,* more Secretly and Powerfully to Undermine Us."[26]

In *The Danger of Priestcraft to Religion and Government* (1702), Dennis sensibly demonstrates the weaknesses of *The Political Union.* He first establishes what he finds to be Sacheverell's design, "to take off the Act of Toleration, and to advance the Temporal Power of the Church: which would not fail to divide and weaken us more and more, and make our Condition desperate" (*SW,* 1:359). He proceeds to criticize the two parts of the proposition. "That Religion is the Grand Support of Government" is not proven, he argues, because for Sacheverell religion is priestcraft, "an Art by which designing Men, in order to their own Advantage, make that pass for Religion upon the unthinking part of the World, that is neither dictated by the Law of Nature, nor included in the written Religion of the Country" (*SW,* 1:361). The main proofs here are the man's lack of charity and disregard for real unity. Dennis seems notably astute in pointing out the "Rancour and Venom" in his opponent's furious diction.

The second part of the proposition Dennis refutes by redefinition of its terms and by examples. He finds his opponent hoping that the king will gain unlawful absolute power when a corrupt clergy make the people accept such "wretched abominable Doctrines" as passive obedience. If the proposition were granted, both the government and the Church would incur ridicule and chaos.

Dennis effectively combines close reading, clear structure, fair examples, and a balanced tone. His argument proved able and popular enough that Sacheverell attacked the "silly Pamphlet" in *The New Association . . . Occasion'd by a Late Pamphlet, Entituled, "The Danger of Priest-Craft"* (1702), a sorry case of illogic and misquotation. The priest never forsook his principles and ironically received in 1713 a fine reward, the living of St. Andrew's, Holborn—Dennis's home parish.

The actions of priests like Sacheverell led to a flood of anticlerical writings, so that by the early 1700s "priestcraft" was a derisive term. Mandeville, Tutchin, Defoe, and hundreds of other authors maintained the pressure on their readers to watch how scheming priests kept religion mysterious and used their pulpits for political ends. In *Priestcraft Distinguish'd from Christianity* (1715), Dennis returns to the topic with a generalized anticlerical sermon that, given its timing, could apply equally well to both Sacheverell and Jacobite clergy.

The subtitle adequately clarifies Dennis's aims: "I. That Wicked *Priests* are the real *Antichrists* mention'd in *Scripture.* II. That the Corruptions of the *Laity* in all *Christian States,* proceeds from the Corruptions of the *Clergy.* III. That there was a more *General Vertue* in the grossest Times of *Paganism,* than there has been since our SAVIOUR came into the World. IV. That there is a more *General Vertue* in other Parts . . . than in the *Christian World.* V. That there was a more *General Vertue* in . . . the Times of our *Ancestors,* than . . . in our *own Times;* and that *Priestcraft,* and *Corruption of Manners,* have increas'd together."[27]

Within his text Dennis reaffirms some of his best material from the 1702 pamphlet. He surely has in mind Sacheverell when he writes, " 'Tis not their business to preach up Charity, or to teach Humility, or any of the Virtues that produce or maintain Charity; as Gentleness, Meekness, Patience, Forbearance, Peace-making, Mercy, Long-suffering, and Forgiveness. . . . Their Business is to preach Division . . ." (*SW,* 2:387). When priests who show no charity and pervert the Gospel gain power, the result must be the social and moral chaos outlined in *The Danger of Priestcraft* and *An Essay upon Publick Spirit.*

Priestcraft Distinguish'd did not succeed with the public. For one thing, it repeats too much from the earlier pamphlet. It works also as an exercise in ponderous logic, not a colorful attack on one specified target. However, Dennis admirably keeps to the moderate tone found later in lines to Blackmore: "There is no Man alive who is less a Friend to Priestcraft than my self . . . But I shall never endeavour to destroy Religion in order to hurt Priestcraft: I know the Balance of right Reason better" (*OL,* 2:467). This self-control is indeed rare in contemporary religious debate.

   Translations of Thomas Burnet.   In his later years Dennis worked lovingly on the religious thought of Thomas Burnet, Master of the Charterhouse, best known for *The Sacred Theory of the Earth.* Dennis admired Burnet even if he did not accept his more curious ideas—for instance, that the Earth before the Deluge was a huge eggshell. Burnet was, after all, a strong Williamite; he was the first to preach before the king after the Revolution, he served William as chaplain-in-ordinary, and he dedicated the 1691 edition of *The Sacred Theory* to William as defender of philosophical liberties.

   In religious matters he was greatly influenced by such Low Churchmen as More and Tillotson, he supported toleration, and his questioning of traditional biblical interpretations in *The Sacred Theory* and *Archaeologiae Philosophicae* made High Church writers brand him a heretic. Dennis also found much to admire in his general way of thinking. Scholars have noted Burnet's hint of sublimity in finding the Alps "too big for our comprehension, they fill and over-bear the mind with their Excess, and cast it into a pleasing kind of stupor and admiration." But Dennis is perhaps even more thrilled by Burnet's always pushing implications of new thoughts as far as he can: "There is no Chase so pleasant, methinks, as to drive a Thought, by good conduct, from one end of the World to the other; and never to lose sight of it till it fall into Eternity, where all things are lost as to our knowledge."[28]

   In 1728 (?) Dennis published *The Faith and Duties of Christians,* his translation of Burnet's *De fide et officiis Christianorum.* He explains in his preface that he has undertaken the 280-page task (no small matter for an aging man with vision problems) because the author's executor asked him, and the treatise can increase public morality. Dennis finds congenial Burnet's temperament in his praise of charity, "without which Christ has declar'd, that the most extraordinary Gifts and Endowments, and the most wonderful Virtues, are of no Significance, much less deserving of Heaven." And we often sense toleration, even universalism: "Nor can I be of Opinion, that even the Doctrine of any particular Church whatever, is entirely purg'd and purified from all Petulancy; but 'tis less erroneous in some Churches than others, and the Errors are fewer, and less important."[29]

Dennis translated Burnet's *De statu mortuorum et resurgentium* as *A Treatise Concerning the State of Departed Souls* (1730). This he felt prompted to do by the "low and vile Buffoonry" of Matthias Earbery, who in 1727–28 perpetrated for Curll a botched translation capitalizing on Burnet's notoriety and ridiculing Burnet in the notes. Earbery's style gives no idea of the original author's much-praised flowing sentences. Dennis, in contrast, maintains the fine style through intricate discussions of our future immortal substance, the interval between death and the Resurrection, the Millennium, and the nature of Heaven and Hell. He catches Burnet's sweeping vision: "Behold the Messiah coming in the Clouds of Heaven, the World in Flames on every Side, and the Dead with Amazement rising, and the Tribunal prepared for the great Day of Judgment. If ever since the Beginning of Time there were, if ever to the End of the World there will be astonishing Scenes, astonishing Sights, such these will transcendently be. Then new Heavens, and a new Earth, will succeed; then the millennary Empire of Christ; and, lastly, the End of this Globe of Earth, and the Consummation of all that belongs to it."[30]

Dennis favors a Christianity that will unify and strengthen the nation as it embraces disparate Protestant beliefs. He defends it firmly yet moderately. The Christian pamphlets well illustrate his wish to serve the public interest.

Through his varied noncritical pamphlets, Dennis writes always as a humanitarian. Gravely concerned about the well-being of his nation and its people, he may write now with righteous anger, now with satiric lightness, now with serenity. But he is always the combined idealist and knowledgeable pragmatist ready to look outside belles lettres and directly help his fellow citizens achieve something like that perfection for which he himself yearns. Not to know this Dennis is not to know Dennis.

Chapter Seven

Toward an Appreciation of Dennis

John Dennis's reputation has encountered three major problems since 1700. First is the logic that we need not seriously consider an author with an objectionable personality. Indeed, the very terms used by many critics to describe our author automatically suspend further thought. We need see only a partial list to sense the animosity: "crusty," "sour old," "irascible," "abusive," "unrelenting," "malicious," "despotic pedantry," "pedantic criticism," "notorious," "paranoid," "almost insane shower of abuse," "butcherly," "furious," "perverted," "waspish," "Grub Street Timon," "cross-grained," "ill-tempered," "of tomahawk critical notoriety." Given its initial strong impulse by Pope, this tradition culminated in *The Calamities and Quarrels of Authors* (1881) of Isaac Disraeli, who argues that the innately evil Dennis made criticism an act of insanity. Fortunately, such an attitude came up against the more objective methods of scholars like William Roberts, author of the 1888 *Dictionary of National Biography* article, the first important modern discussion of our author. Since then, serious critics have at least paid him the respect of reading him before judging his work.

A closely related problem is neglect of Dennis's texts. As early as 1776 Johnson averred that the critical works should be collected. Robert Southey voiced the same hope in 1807 and J. E. Spingarn in 1899. However, readers had to wait until 1939 and 1943, when Edward Niles Hooker published the two splendid volumes of *The Critical Works of John Dennis.* This work, with its full introduction and notes, may forever remain the standard edition of the criticism. In his other writings Dennis has been much less fortunate. We can get facsimile reprints in, for example, the University Microfilms formats, the "Early English Books, 1641–1700" microform series, and the 1980

Garland edition of the plays. But except for isolated instances, such as *The Reverse* and *Appius and Virginia,* we cannot find these writings in texts edited by modern standards and made more useful by full scholarly commentary. Obviously, a continuing inquiry into Dennis's work depends in large part upon the publication of these works in sound critical editions.

Contemporary renown as "the Critic" and the lack of modern texts have helped create the third problem, the rather myopic view of Dennis as only a critic. Perhaps the strongest contributing factor is one overriding truth: much of his literary criticism is indeed more significant than his other writings. He contributed greatly to such future critical trends as associationism and relativism. He had much to do with Arnold's praise of action in narrative poetry, many of Gildon's critical views, Goldsmith's opinions about the working of religion in poetry and the place of low characters in comedy, Addison's criticism of Milton, Johnson's work on Addison, Shaftesbury's emphasis upon taste, Watts's theorizing on religion and poetry, and Wordsworth's thoughts on passion. And he at least anticipates many ideas elaborated upon by Burke, Hazlitt, Keats, and Shelley. Not surprisingly, such outstanding critics as Louis I. Bredvold, Giles Jacob, John Loftis, and H. T. Swedenberg, Jr., unite in judging Dennis the finest critic of his age.

But we lose valuable perspectives on Dennis when we focus solely on his criticism. Thus many aesthetically sophisticated analyses of his criticism sound depressingly like pastiches of quotations from the *Critical Works.* Even critics professedly analyzing his plays often merely cite his statements on dramatic technique.

How much easier and more fulfilling our evaluations may become if we see Dennis as a whole person. We find him, for example, always deeply committed to truth because he feels that he is right. Writing in 1725, he insists that his reputation for ill nature derives solely from battles for liberty and against false art. (*OL,* 1:203–4) The foe might be King Louis, Sacheverell, Law, Jacobites, Pope, theatrical acrobats, brutal sea captains—someone who through illogic, selfishness, lust for power, or ignorance is threatening to destroy order. To restore literary, social, religious, or political order, he attacks with a style that over the years becomes more unrelenting than that found in most controversialists of his day. But he has the sometimes bull-headed integrity to keep hammering when he feels that he must, regardless of how his approach might irritate readers.

When we analyze individual works from this wider perspective, we might ask some interesting questions. For instance, why is *The Reverse* so much stronger poetically than the turgid and bombastic verses that Dennis reprinted in the *Select Works?* A full answer could involve his dedication to public service, "which has been all along the darling Passion of my Life" (*OL,* 2:358); his early realization that he cannot fulfill his social obligations by being only a critic; his willingness to experiment; his gift of controversialists' strategy; his inability to create sheerly imaginative literature.

Such criticism has not really begun, although it should. John Dennis is an interesting figure whose career affords fine opportunities for meaningful research and analysis. His life with its changes of direction and its obscurities, his overall philosophy of politics and literature, his plays with their many flat moments and some moments of telling strategy, his surprisingly varied nonliterary pamphlets, his oftentimes unsure but valiant attempts at poetry—all await the full evaluation that they deserve.

Notes and References

Chapter One

1. Valuable biographical sources include David Erskine Baker, *The Companion to the Play-House,* 2 vols. (London: T. Becket & P. A. Dehondt et al., 1764); Theophilus Cibber, *The Lives of the Poets of Great Britain and Ireland,* 5 vols. (London: R. Griffiths, 1753); Giles Jacob, *The Poetical Register,* 2 vols. (London, 1719–20); Andrew Kippis, *Biographia Britannica,* 2d ed., 5 vols. (London, 1778–93); Hermann Lenz, *John Dennis: Sein Leben und Seine Werke* (Marburg, 1913); *The Life of Mr. John Dennis* (London, 1734); H. G. Paul, *John Dennis: His Life and Criticism* (1911; reprint, New York, 1966); William Roberts, "John Dennis," *Dictionary of National Biography;* Pat Rogers, "New Light on John Dennis," *Notes and Queries* 19 (1972):217–18; Fred S. Tupper, "Notes on the Life of John Dennis," *ELH* 5 (1938):211–17; Thomas Whincop, *Scanderbeg. . . . To Which Are Added a List of All the Dramatic Authors* (London, 1747). See also from Dennis's works: *The Critical Works,* ed. Edward Niles Hooker, 2 vols. (Baltimore, 1939–43); *Letters upon Several Occasions* (London, 1696); *Miscellanies in Verse and Prose* (London, 1693); *Original Letters,* 2 vols. (London, 1721); *The Select Works,* 2 vols. (London, 1718).

2. Richard B. Kline, "Prior and Dennis," *Notes and Queries* 13 (1966):216.

3. John Venn and J. A. Venn, eds., *Alumni Cantabrigienses: A Biographical List of All Known Students, Graduates . . . to 1900,* part I, 4 vols. (1922–27; reprint, New York: Kraus Reprint, 1974), 2:32.

4. Tupper, "Notes," p. 212.

5. *The Poems of Jonathan Swift,* ed. Harold Williams, 2d ed., 3 vols. (Oxford: Clarendon Press, 1958), 1:184, 3:1098.

6. Cibber, *Lives,* 4:235.

7. [James Miller,] *Harlequin-Horace: or, The Art of Modern Poetry* (*1731*), intro. Antony Coleman, Augustan Reprint Society, no. 178 (Los Angeles: William Andrews Clark Memorial Library, 1976), p. 58; *The Grub-street Journal,* no. 78 (1 July 1731).

8. Terence P. Logan, "John Dennis's *Select Works,* 1718, 1721," *Papers of the Bibliographical Society of America* 65 (1971):155–56.

Chapter Two

1. See Martin C. Battestin, *The Providence of Wit: Aspects of Form in Augustan Literature and the Arts* (Oxford: Clarendon Press, 1974), pp. 51–55.
2. William Godwin, *Lives of Edward and John Philips* (London: Longman et al., 1815), p. 293.
3. The fullest discussion is Edward Richeson, Jr., "John Dennis as a Psychological Critic" (Ph.D. diss., Boston University, 1962).
4. Clarence DeWitt Thorpe makes interesting comments in "Two Augustans Cross the Alps: Dennis and Addison on Mountain Scenery," *Studies in Philology* 32 (1935):463–82. Other helpful discussions of Dennis and the sublime include W. P. Albrecht, "John Dennis and the Sublime Pleasures of Tragedy," *Studies on Voltaire and the Eighteenth Century* 87 (1972):65–85; Samuel H. Monk, *The Sublime: A Study of Critical Theories in XVIII-Century England* (1935; reprint, Ann Arbor, 1960), pp. 45–54; Marjorie Hope Nicolson, *Mountain Gloom and Mountain Glory: The Development of the Aesthetics of the Infinite* (1959; reprint, New York, 1963), pp. 276–89.
5. Longinus, *On the Sublime,* in T. S. Dorsch, trans., *Classical Literary Criticism* (Harmondsworth: Penguin, 1965), pp. 108–53.
6. John Gay, *The Mohocks* (London: Bernard Lintott, 1712), sig. A2.
7. H. James Jensen cryptically makes such an observation in *The Muses' Concord: Literature, Music, and the Visual Arts in the Baroque Age* (Bloomington: Indiana University Press, 1976), pp. 161–62.

Chapter Three

1. The best concise introduction to Dennis's Milton criticism is John T. Shawcross, "John Dennis," in *A Milton Encyclopedia,* ed. William B. Hunter et al., 8 vols. (Lewisburg, Pa., 1978–80), 2:141–43.
2. Vereen M. Bell, "Johnson's Milton Criticism in Context," *English Studies* 49 (1968):127–32.
3. Helpful discussions include Sister Rose Anthony, *The Jeremy Collier Stage Controversy* (1937; reprint, New York: Benjamin Blom, 1966); *CW,* 1:466–70; Joseph Wood Krutch, *Comedy and Conscience after the Restoration* (New York: Columbia University Press, 1924); J. E. Spingarn, ed., *Critical Essays of the Seventeenth Century,* 3 vols. (1908–9; reprint ed., Bloomington: Indiana University Press, 1957), 1:lxxxi–lxxxvii; A. J. Turner, "The Jeremy Collier Stage Controversy Again," *Notes and Queries* 20 (1973):409–12.

4. See J. Hopes, "Politics and Morality in the Writings of Jeremy Collier," *Literature and History* 8 (1978):159–74.

5. See also Anthony, *Collier,* p. 97; D. Crane Taylor, *William Congreve* (Oxford: Clarendon Press, 1931), p. 126.

6. Arthur Bedford, *The Evil and Danger of Stage-Plays* (Bristol: W. Bonny, 1706), p. 2.

7. Jeremy Collier, *A Defence of the Short View* (London: S. Keble et al., 1699), p. 137.

8. William Law, *The Absolute Unlawfulness of the Stage-Entertainment Fully Demonstrated* (London: W. and J. Innys, 1726), pp. 44–45, 3–4.

9. J. H. Overton, *William Law, Nonjuror and Mystic* (London: Longmans, Green, & Co., 1881), p. 37. See also Arthur W. Hopkinson, *About William Law* (London: Society for Promoting Christian Knowledge, 1948), p. 31; A. Keith Walker, *William Law: His Life and Thought* (London: Society for Promoting Christian Knowledge, 1973), p. 41.

10. "Mrs. S—— O——," in *Law Outlaw'd: or, A Short Reply to Mr. Law's Long Declamation against the Stage* (London: Booksellers of London and Westminster, 1726), title page.

11. *The Critical Works of Thomas Rymer,* ed. Curt A. Zimansky (New Haven: Yale University Press, 1956), p. 127.

12. Daniel Kenrick, *A New Session of the Poets* (London: A. Baldwin, 1700), p. 3.

13. *The Poetics of Aristotle in England,* Cornell Studies in English, no. 17 (New Haven: Yale University Press, for Cornell University, 1930), p. 84.

14. *Remarks on a Book Entituled, Prince Arthur, an Heroick Poem* (London, 1696), sig. *lv.

15. H. T. Swedenberg, Jr., *The Theory of the Epic in England 1650–1800* (1944; reprint, New York: Russell & Russell, 1972), p. 54.

16. For biographical details see Peter Smithers, *The Life of Joseph Addison,* 2d ed. (Oxford: Clarendon Press, 1968).

17. *Spectator,* ed. Donald F. Bond, 5 vols. (Oxford: Clarendon Press, 1965), 1:168–69. On the two critics' opposing ideas about poetic justice, see Lee Andrew Elioseff, *The Cultural Milieu of Addison's Literary Criticism* (Austin: University of Texas Press, 1963), pp. 85–92; M. A. Quinlan, *Poetic Justice in the Drama* (Notre Dame: University Press, 1912).

18. *Spectator,* 4:463–64.

19. M. M. Kelsall provides the best analysis of the popular response to Addison's symbolism in "The Meaning of Addison's *Cato,*" *Review of English Studies* 17 (1966):149–62.

20. *Tracts and Pamphlets by Richard Steele,* ed. Rae Blanchard (Baltimore: Johns Hopkins Press, 1944), pp. 61, 172.

21. For insightful comments on Dennis's and Steele's relations, see especially John Loftis, *Steele at Drury Lane* (Berkeley and Los Angeles: University of California Press, 1952), pp. 163–69, 203–11; *CW,* 2:xxxi–xxxiv.

22. *Richard Steele's "The Theatre" 1720,* ed. John Loftis (Oxford: Clarendon Press, 1962), pp. 47, 53.

23. *The Battle of the Authors Lately Fought in Covent-Garden, between Sir John Edgar, Generalissimo on One Side, and Horatius Truewit, on the Other* (London: J. Roberts, 1720), p. 7.

24. *A Defence of Sir Fopling Flutter* (London, 1722), title page. See Shirley Strum Kenny, "Richard Steele and the 'Pattern of Genteel Comedy,' " *Modern Philology* 70 (1972):22–37.

25. *Spectator,* 1:278–79.

26. *The Plays of Richard Steele,* ed. Shirley Strum Kenny (Oxford: Clarendon Press, 1971), p. 300.

27. John Loftis, ed., *Essays on the Theatre from Eighteenth-Century Periodicals,* Augustan Reprint Society, no. 85–86 (Los Angeles: William Andrews Clark Memorial Library, 1960), p. 27.

28. Two of the most helpful guides to the relations between Dennis and Pope are Joseph V. Guerinot, *Pamphlet Attacks on Alexander Pope 1711–1744: A Descriptive Bibliography* (London: Methuen, 1969); *The Poems of Alexander Pope* (Twickenham Edition), ed. John Butt et al., 11 vols. in 12 (London: Methuen and New Haven: Yale University Press, 1936–69).

29. Charles Gildon, *Memoirs of the Life of William Wycherley* (London: E. Curll, 1718), p. 15.

30. *The Correspondence of Alexander Pope,* ed. George Sherburn, 5 vols. (Oxford: Clarendon Press, 1956), 1:69, 136, 27.

31. Pope, *Poems,* 1:270, 306–7. On the Appius reference, see A. N. Wilkins, "Pope and 'Appius,' " *Notes and Queries* 7 (1960):292–94.

32. Owen Ruffhead, *The Life of Alexander Pope* (London: C. Bathurst et al., 1769), p. 98; Robert Kilburn Root, *The Poetical Career of Alexander Pope* (Princeton: Princeton University Press, 1938), p. 22.

33. *The Prose Works of Alexander Pope,* ed. Norman Ault (Oxford: Basil Blackwell, 1936), pp. 3–18, 153–68.

34. Pope, *Prose Works,* pp. 13, 16, 5.

35. George Sherburn, *The Early Career of Alexander Pope* (1934; reprint, New York: Russell & Russell, 1963), p. 106.

36. Pope, *Prose Works,* pp. 162, 167.

37. E. N. Hooker supplies convincing evidence for Dennis's authorship in "Pope and Dennis," *ELH* 7 (1940):188–98.

38. Joseph V. Guerinot, intro., *Two Poems against Pope,* Augustan Reprint Society, no. 114 (Los Angeles: University of California Press, 1965), p. 5.

39. Alexander Pope, *The Art of Sinking in Poetry: Martinus Scriblerus' Peri Bathous,* ed. Edna Leake Steeves (1952; reprint, New York: Russell & Russell, 1962), pp. 27, 53, 88–89.

40. Geoffrey Tillotson comments on the pamphlet and Pope's annotations in his copy in Pope, *Poems,* 2:392–99.

41. Alan T. McKenzie, "The Solemn Owl and the Laden Ass: The Iconography of the Frontispieces to *The Dunciad,"* *Harvard Library Bulletin* 24 (1976):25–39; Pope, *Poems,* 5:240.

42. Pope, *Poems,* 5:128.

43. Ibid., 5:72–75, 167.

44. Edmund Curll, *A Compleat Key to the Dunciad* (London: A. Dodd, 1728), pp. iii–iv.

45. Pope, *Correspondence,* 3:357–58; Pope, *Poems,* 6:355–56.

Chapter Four

1. *A Plot, and No Plot* (London, 1697), sig. A 4v.

2. *Life of Mr. John Dennis,* p. 20.

3. This pamphlet is reprinted in Herbert Davis, intro., "Musical Entertainments in *Rinaldo and Armida:* by John Dennis," in *Theatre Miscellany: Six Pieces Connected with the Seventeenth-Century Stage,* Luttrell Society Reprints, no. 14 (Oxford, 1953), pp. 97–115.

4. *Rinaldo and Armida* (London, 1699), sig. a4.

5. M. A. Shaaber, "A Letter from Mrs. Barry," *Library Chronicle* 16 (1950):46.

6. *Iphigenia* (London, 1700), sig. A3.

7. H. D. F. Kitto, *Greek Tragedy: A Literary Study* (1952; reprint, Garden City, N.Y.: Doubleday, 1954), p. 332.

8. Cibber, *Lives,* 4:233; Kippis, *Biographia,* 5:102.

9. John Downes, *Roscius Anglicanus,* intro. John Loftis, Augustan Reprint Society, no. 134 (Los Angeles: William Andrews Clark Memorial Library, 1969), p. 45.

10. Abel Boyer, *Achilles: or, Iphigenia in Aulis* (London: Tho. Bennet, 1700), sig. A3.

11. For other analyses of *Iphigenia,* see A. Hirt, "A Question of Excess: Neo-Classical Adaptations of Greek Tragedy," *Costerus* 3 (1972):55–119; William Henry Ingram, "Greek Drama and the Au-

gustan Stage: Dennis, Theobald, Thomson" (Ph.D. diss., University of Pennsylvania, 1966).

12. See A. N. Wilkins, "Tragedy and 'The True Politicks,'" *Notes and Queries* 204 (1959):390–94.

13. See, e.g., *The Life of Mr. John Dennis,* pp. 22–23.

14. John Loftis, *The Politics of Drama in Augustan England* (Oxford: Clarendon Press, 1963), p. 42; *The Letters of Joseph Addison,* ed. Walter Graham (Oxford: Clarendon Press, 1941), p. 49.

15. Jacob, *Poetical Register,* 1:286.

16. *Gibraltar: or, The Spanish Adventure* (London, 1705), p. 24. The pages misnumbered 49–72 are silently corrected to 57–80.

17. Robert Hume, *The Development of English Drama in the Late Seventeenth Century* (Oxford: Clarendon Press, 1976), p. 471.

18. Useful discussions are Frederick S. Boas, *An Introduction to Eighteenth-Century Drama 1700–1780* (Oxford: Clarendon Press, 1953), pp. 144–49; Arthur Norman Wilkins, "An Essay on John Dennis's Theory and Practice of the Art of Tragedy Together with the Text of His Tragedy of *Appius and Virginia*" (Ph.D. diss., Washington University, 1953).

19. John Gay, *The Mohocks,* sig. A2 and p. 4.

20. See A. N. Wilkins, "John Dennis' Stolen Thunder," *Notes and Queries* 201 (1956):425–28.

21. See especially Charles Beecher Hogan, *Shakespeare in the Theatre 1701–1800,* 2 vols. (Oxford: Clarendon Press, 1952–57), 1:319; Hazelton Spencer, *Shakespeare Improved: The Restoration Versions in Quarto and on the Stage* (1927; reprint, New York: Frederick Ungar, 1963), pp. 346–49.

22. *The Comical Gallant* (London, 1702), p. 43.

23. See J. A. Bryant, Jr., "Falstaff and the Renewal of Windsor," *PMLA* 89 (1974):296–301.

24. *The Merry Wives of Windsor* 3.5.35–37. All Shakespeare quotations come from *The Riverside Shakespeare,* ed. G. Blakemore Evans et al. (Boston: Houghton Mifflin, 1974).

25. *Merry Wives* 5.5.241–43.

26. Spencer, *Shakespeare Improved,* p. 347.

27. *A Comparison between the Two Stages,* ed. Staring B. Wells (Princeton: Princeton University Press, 1942), p. 97; Baker, *Companion,* 1:sig. E1r-v; Herbert Spencer Robinson, *English Shakesperian Criticism in the Eighteenth Century* (New York: H. W. Wilson, 1932), p. 9; Montague Summers, *The Playhouse of Pepys* (1935; reprint, New York: Humanities Press, 1964), p. 310; Spencer, *Shakespeare Improved,* pp. 349–50.

28. *The Invader of His Country: or, The Fatal Resentment* (London, 1720), sig. A7.

29. George C. Branam, *Eighteenth-Century Adaptations of Shakespearean Tragedy,* University of California Publications, English Studies (Berkeley and Los Angeles: University of California Press, 1956), 14:22. Helpful summaries of Dennis's changes in the scenes are Hogan, *Shakespeare in the Theatre,* p. 100; George C. D. Odell, *Shakespeare from Betterton to Irving,* 2 vols. (New York: Charles Scribner's Sons, 1920), 1:239–41.

30. *Coriolanus* 2.1.169–75.

31. Gail Kern Paster, "To Starve with Feeding: The City in *Coriolanus,*" *Shakespeare Studies* 11 (1978):143.

Chapter Five

1. *Pendragon: or, The Carpet Knight His Kalendar* (London: J. Newton, 1698), sig. A4.

2. *Poems in Burlesque* (London, 1692), sig. A2v.

3. Edward Ames Richards, *Hudibras in the Burlesque Tradition* (1937; reprint, New York: Octagon, 1972), p. 163; David Farley-Hills, *The Benevolence of Laughter: Comic Poetry of the Commonwealth and Restoration* (Totowa, N.J.: Rowman & Littlefield, 1974), pp. 47–48.

4. *Gentleman's Journal,* November 1692, p. 2.

5. John S. Shea succinctly examines Dennis's treatment of La Fontaine in his introduction to Bernard Mandeville, *AEsop Dress'd or a Collection of Fables Writ in Familiar Verse (1704),* Augustan Reprint Society, no. 120 (Los Angeles: William Andrews Clark Memorial Library, 1966).

6. *Miscellanies in Verse and Prose* (London, 1693), p. 26.

7. Thomas Middleton Raysor, ed., *Coleridge's Shakespearean Criticism* (London: Constable, 1930), 2:44.

8. The most detailed survey of the earlier Marlborough literature is Robert D. Horn, *Marlborough: A Survey: Panegyrics, Satires, and Biographical Writings, 1688–1788* (New York: Garland, 1974).

9. Cibber, *Lives,* 4:217.

10. *The Mourning Poets* (London: n.p., 1695), p. 11.

11. Guy Miege, *The New State of England. Under Our Present Monarch King William III* (London: R. Clavel et al., 1699), part II, p. 100.

12. See Earl Miner, intro., *Poems on the Reign of William III,* Augustan Reprint Society, no. 166 (Los Angeles: William Andrews Clark Memorial Library, 1974), pp. ii–xi.

13. See David Green, *Queen Anne* (New York: Charles Scribner's Sons, 1970), p. 335.

14. Cibber, *Lives,* 4:236; Kippis, *Biographia,* 5:100.

15. John Tutchin, *The Foreigners,* ll. 81–85. Quotations from *The Foreigners* and *The Reverse* are from the parallel texts in *Poems on Affairs of State: Augustan Satirical Verse, 1660–1714,* general ed. George deF. Lord (New Haven, 1963–75), 6:224–47.

16. Edward Ward, *The Secret History of the Calves-Head Clubb, or, the Republican Unmasqu'd* (London: Booksellers of London and Westminster, 1703), p. 10.

17. John Tutchin, *The Foreigners,* ll. 134–35.

18. John Tutchin, *The Apostates* (London: M. Fabian, 1701), p. 12.

Chapter Six

1. Roger Fiske, *English Theatre Music in the Eighteenth Century* (London: Oxford University Press, 1973), p. 3.

2. Charles Gildon, *The Life of Mr. Thomas Betterton* (London: R. Gosling, 1710), p. 169.

3. Cited in Emmett L. Avery, "Vaudeville on the London Stage, 1700–1737," *Research Studies of the State College of Washington* 5 (1937):67.

4. Kippis, *Biographia,* 5:107.

5. See Howard D. Weinbrot, *Augustas Caesar in "Augustan" England: The Decline of a Classical Norm* (Princeton: Princeton University Press, 1978).

6. *Julius Caesar Acquitted* (London, 1722), p. 3.

7. Helpful discussions of *The Fable* include Thomas R. Edwards, Jr., "Mandeville's Moral Prose," *ELH* 31 (1964):195–212; Phillip Harth, "The Satiric Purpose of *The Fable of the Bees,*" *Eighteenth-Century Studies* 2 (1969):321–40; Hector Monro, *The Ambivalence of Bernard Mandeville* (Oxford: Clarendon Press, 1975).

8. Bernard Mandeville, *The Fable of the Bees: Or, Private Vices, Publick Benefits,* ed. F. B. Kaye (Oxford: Clarendon Press, 1924), 1:42.

9. *Vice and Luxury Publick Mischiefs: or, Remarks on a Book Intituled, The Fable of the Bees; or, Private Vices Publick Benefits* (London, 1724), pp. iv, xvi.

10. Bernard Mandeville, *A Letter to Dion, Occasion'd by His Book Call'd Alciphron,* intro. Jacob Viner, Augustan Reprint Society, no. 41 (Los Angeles: William Andrews Clark Memorial Library, 1953), pp. 31–32.

11. For helpful modern discussions of naval problems, see especially Daniel A. Baugh, *British Naval Administration in the Age of Walpole* (Princeton: Princeton University Press, 1965); John Ehrman, *The Navy in the War of William III 1689–1697: Its State and Direction* (Cambridge: Cambridge University Press, 1953); Peter Kemp, *The British Sailor: A Social History of the Lower Deck* (London: J. M. Dent & Sons, 1970); Christopher Lloyd, *The British Seaman 1200–1860: A Social Survey* (Rutherford, N.J.: Fairleigh Dickinson University Press, 1970).

12. *The Journals of the House of Commons,* 13:124.

13. *An Essay on the Navy* (London, 1702).

14. *A Rough Draught of a New Model at Sea,* in *Select Naval Documents,* ed. H. W. Hodges and E. A. Hughes (Cambridge: Cambridge University Press, 1922), p. 109.

15. *The Letters of Daniel Defoe,* ed. George Harris Healey (Oxford: Clarendon Press, 1955), p. 73.

16. Thomas Robe, *Ways and Means Whereby His Majesty May Man His Navy with Ten Thousand Able Sailors* (London: J. Roberts, 1726), p. 16.

17. We can gauge the magnitude of the problem by noting popular tunes like "The Sailor's Complaint" and "The Sailor's Garland; or, the Ticket Buyer's Lamentation," in *Naval Songs and Ballads,* ed. C. H. Firth (London: Navy Records Society, 1908), pp. 230–32.

18. Robert Crosfeild, *Justice Perverted, and Innocence & Loyalty Oppressed* (London: n.p., 1695), p. 16.

19. Kemp remarks that *An Essay on the Navy* "contains the first mention of the nine-tailed cat, that vicious instrument of punishment" (p. 59).

20. Ehrman, *Navy,* p. 128.

21. See Robe, *Ways and Means;* Alexander Justice, *A General Treatise of the Dominion and Laws of the Sea* (London: S. & J. Sprint et al., 1705), pp. 626, 653–57; Peter Rowe, *A True Method* (London: n.p., 1703), p. 4.

22. Herbert Richmond, *Statesmen and Sea Power* (Oxford: Clarendon Press, 1946), p. 69.

23. Ralph Davis, *The Rise of the English Shipping Industry in the Seventeenth and Eighteenth Centuries* (London: Macmillan, 1962), p. 25.

24. *A Proposal for Putting a Speedy End to the War* (London, 1703), p. viii.

25. "Articles of Impeachment against Henry Sacheverell," in David C. Douglas, ed., *English Historical Documents* (New York: Oxford University Press, 1953–), 8:206.

26. Henry Sacheverell, *The Political Union* (Oxford: George West & Henry Clements, 1702), pp. 5, 49–50, 61.

27. *Priestcraft Distinguish'd from Christianity* (London, 1715), title page.

28. Thomas Burnet, *The Sacred Theory of the Earth,* intro. Basil Willey (Carbondale: Southern Illinois University Press, 1965), pp. 110, 26.

29. *The Faith and Duties of Christians* (London, 1728), pp. 143, 271.

30. *A Treatise Concerning the State of Departed Souls before, and at, and after the Resurrection* (London, 1730), p. 125.

Selected Bibliography

PRIMARY SOURCES

1. Selected and Collected Writings

The Critical Works of John Dennis. Edited by Edward Niles Hooker. 2 vols. Baltimore: Johns Hopkins Press, 1939–43. Splendid edition of all but a few isolated pages of the critical writings. Contains a thoughtful introduction placing Dennis within the critical context of his age; invaluable, full notes; thoroughly indexed.

Miscellaneous Tracts. Vol. 1 (no more published). London: The author, 1727.

Miscellanies in Verse and Prose. London: James Knapton, 1693.

Miscellany Poems. . . . The Second Edition with Large Additions. London: Sam. Briscoe, 1697. An expanded version of the *Miscellanies.*

The Plays of John Dennis. Edited by J. W. Johnson. New York: Garland, 1980. Facsimile reprints of all the plays except the Shakespearean adaptations and the masque.

Poems and Letters upon Several Occasions. London: D. Brown, 1692.

The Select Works of Mr. John Dennis. 2 vols. London: John Darby, 1718.

2. Critical Writings

The Advancement and Reformation of Modern Poetry. London: Rich. Parker, 1701.

The Characters and Conduct of Sir John Edgar, Call'd by Himself Sole Monarch of the Stage in Drury-Lane; and His Three Deputy-Governors. In Two Letters to Sir John Edgar. London: M. Smith, 1720.

The Characters and Conduct of Sir John Edgar. . . . In a Third and Fourth Letter to the Knight. London: J. Roberts, 1720.

A Defence of Sir Fopling Flutter, a Comedy Written by Sir George Etheridge. London: T. Warner, 1722.

An Essay on the Genius and Writings of Shakespear: with Some Letters of Criticism to the Spectator. London: Bernard Lintott, 1712.

The Grounds of Criticism in Poetry, Contain'd in Some New Discoveries Never Made Before, Requisite for the Writing and Judging of Poems Surely. London: Geo. Strahan & Bernard Lintott, 1704.

The Impartial Critick: or, Some Observations upon a Late Book, Entituled, A Short View of Tragedy, Written by Mr. Rymer. London: R. Taylor, 1693.

"Musical Entertainments in *Rinaldo and Armida:* by John Dennis." Introduction by Herbert Davis. In *Theatre Miscellany: Six Pieces Connected with the Seventeenth-Century Stage.* Luttrell Society Reprints, no. 14. Oxford: For the Luttrell Society by Basil Blackwell, 1953, pp. 97–115. This is a 1699 collection of the musical numbers in the play, including Dennis's preface (not in Hooker's edition).

"Of Prosody." In 2d ed. of *An Essay towards a Practical English Grammar, Describing the Genius and Nature of the English Tongue,* by James Greenwood. London: John Clark, 1722, pp. 265–71.

The Person of Quality's Answer to Mr. Collier's Letter, Being a Disswasive from the Play-House. London: Booksellers of London & Westminster, 1704.

Prologue for Charles Gildon. *The Patriot, or the Italian Conspiracy.* London: W. Davis et al., 1703.

Prologue for John Oldmixon. *Amintas. . . . Made English out of Italian.* London: Rich. Parker, 1698.

Reflections Critical and Satyrical, upon a Late Rhapsody, Call'd, An Essay upon Criticism. London: Bernard Lintott, [1711].

Remarks on a Book Entituled, Prince Arthur, an Heroick Poem. With Some General Critical Observations, and Several New Remarks upon Virgil. London: S. Heyrick & R. Sare, 1696.

Remarks on a Play, Call'd, The Conscious Lovers, a Comedy. London: T. Warner, 1723.

Remarks on Mr. Pope's Rape of the Lock. London: J. Roberts, 1728.

Remarks upon Cato, a Tragedy. London: B. Lintott, 1713.

Remarks upon Mr. Pope's Translation of Homer. With Two Letters Concerning Windsor Forest, and The Temple of Fame. London: E. Curll, 1717.

Remarks upon Several Passages in the Preliminaries to the Dunciad. . . . And upon Several Passages in Pope's Preface to His Translation of Homer's Iliad. London: H. Whitridge, 1729.

The Stage Defended, from Scripture, Reason, Experience, and the Common Sense of Mankind, for Two Thousand Years. Occasion'd by Mr. Law's Late Pamphlet against Stage-Entertainments. London: N. Blandford, 1726.

A True Character of Mr. Pope, and His Writings. London: Sarah Popping, 1716.

The Usefulness of the Stage, to the Happiness of Mankind. To Government, and to Religion. Occasioned by a Late Book, Written by Jeremy Collier, M.A. London: Rich. Parker, 1698.

3. Noncritical Prose

The Annals and History of Cornelius Tacitus: His Account of the Antient Germans, and the Life of Agricola. Made English by Several Hands. 3 vols. London: Matthew Gillyflower, 1698. Dennis's work is vol. 3, bk. 5.

The Danger of Priestcraft to Religion and Government: with Some Politick Reasons for Toleration. Occasion'd by a Discourse of Mr. Sacheverel's, Intitul'd, The Political Union. London: n.p., 1702.

An Essay on the Navy, or England's Advantage and Safety, Prov'd Dependant on a Formidable and Well-Disciplined Navy; and the Encrease and Encouragement of Seamen. London: John Nutt, 1702.

An Essay on the Opera's after the Italian Manner, Which Are About To Be Establish'd on the English Stage: With Some Reflections on the Damage Which They May Bring to the Publick. London: John Nutt, 1706.

An Essay upon Publick Spirit; Being a Satyr in Prose upon the Manners and Luxury of the Times, the Chief Sources of Our Present Parties and Divisions. London: Bernard Lintott, 1711.

The Faith and Duties of Christians. Translation of *De fide et officiis Christianorum,* by Thomas Burnet. London: J. Hooke, [1728].

Julius Caesar Acquitted, and His Murderers Condemn'd. London: J. MackEuen, 1722.

Priestcraft Distinguish'd from Christianity. London: J. Roberts, 1715.

A Proposal for Putting a Speedy End to the War, by Ruining the Commerce of the French and Spaniards, and Securing Our Own, without Any Additional Expence to the Nation. London: Daniel Brown & Andrew Bell, 1703.

The Seamens Case with Respect to Their Service in the Navy, Wherein Divers Hardships Which They Undergo Are Truly Stated, and Humbly Presented to His Majesty and Both Houses of Parliament. N.p., [ca. 1700].

A Treatise Concerning the State of Departed Souls before, and at, and after the Resurrection. Translation of *De statu mortuorum et resurgentium liber,* by Thomas Burnet. London: John Hooke, 1730.

Vice and Luxury Publick Mischiefs; or, Remarks on a Book Intituled, The Fable of the Bees; or, Private Vices Publick Benefits. London: W. Mears, 1724.

4. Plays

Appius and Virginia. A Tragedy. London: Bernard Lintott, [1709].

The Comical Gallant: or The Amours of Sir John Falstaffe. A Comedy. London: A. Baldwin, 1702.

Gibraltar: or, The Spanish Adventure, a Comedy. London: Wm. Turner, 1705.

The Invader of His Country: or, The Fatal Resentment. A Tragedy. London: J. Pemberton & J. Watts, 1720.

Iphigenia. A Tragedy. London: Richard Parker, 1700.

Liberty Asserted. A Tragedy. London: George Strahan & Bernard Lintott, 1704.

"The Masque of Orpheus and Euridice." In *Muses Mercury: or The Monthly Miscellany,* February 1707, pp. 29–35.

A Plot, and No Plot. A Comedy. London: R. Parker et al., [1697].

Rinaldo and Armida: a Tragedy. London: Jacob Tonson, [1699].

5. Poetry

The Battle of Ramillia: or, The Power of Union. London: Ben. Bragg, 1706.

Britannia Triumphans: or The Empire Sav'd, and Europe Deliver'd. By the Success of Her Majesty's Forces under the Wise and Heroick Conduct of His Grace the Duke of Marlborough. London: J. Nutt, 1704.

The Court of Death. A Pindarique Poem, Dedicated to the Memory of Her Most Sacred Majesty, Queen Mary. London: James Knapton, 1695.

The Monument: a Poem Sacred to the Immortal Memory of the Best and Greatest of Kings, William the Third. London: D. Brown & A. Bell, 1702.

The Nuptials of Britain's Genius and Fame. A Pindaric Poem on the Peace. London: R. Parker & Sam. Briscoe, 1697.

The Passion of Byblis, Made English. London: Rich. Parker, 1692.

A Poem upon the Death of Her Late Sacred Majesty Queen Anne, and the Most Happy and Most Auspicious Accession of His Sacred Majesty King George. London: J. Baker, 1714.

Poems in Burlesque. London: Booksellers of London & Westminster, 1692.

The Reverse: or, The Tables Turn'd. A Poem Written in Answer, Paragraph by Paragraph, to a Late Scurrilous and Malicious Medly of Rhimes Called The Foreigners. London: John Nutt, 1700. Also reprinted in *Poems on Affairs of State: Augustan Satirical Verse, 1660–1714.* General editor George deF. Lord. 7 vols. New Haven: Yale University Press, 1963–75, 6:227–47.

6. Letters

Letters upon Several Occasions: Written by and between Mr. Dryden, Mr. Wycherly, Mr. ———, Mr. Congreve, and Mr. Dennis. London: Sam. Briscoe, 1696.

Original Letters, Familiar, Moral and Critical. 2 vols. London: W. Mears, 1721.

SECONDARY SOURCES

1. Books and Parts of Books

Disraeli, Isaac. *The Calamities and Quarrels of Authors.* 2 vols. in 1. New York: A. C. Armstrong, 1881. Savage attack on Dennis as an ill-tempered critic; repeats several doubtful anecdotes.

Genest, John. *Some Account of the English Stage, from the Restoration in 1660 to 1830.* 10 vols. Bath: H. E. Carrington, 1832. Rather full plot summaries and miscellaneous comments; old but still useful.

Grace, Joan C. *Tragic Theory in the Critical Works of Thomas Rymer, John Dennis, and John Dryden.* Rutherford, N.J.: Fairleigh Dickinson University Press, 1975. A sensitive discussion of Dennis's establishment of genius as the ultimate critical standard, his sympathetic treatment of the passions, and his appreciative response to Shakespeare.

Jacob, Giles. *The Poetical Register: or, The Lives and Characters of All the English Poets.* 2 vols. London: E. Curll, 1719–20. The earliest biographical account; notable for including material supplied by Dennis.

Kippis, Andrew. *Biographia Britannica: or, The Lives of the Most Eminent Persons Who Have Flourished in Great-Britain and Ireland, from the Earliest Ages, to the Present Times.* 2d ed. 5 vols. London: C. Bathurst et al., 1778–93. One of the better eighteenth-century biographical-critical accounts; contains both spurious anecdotes and original critiques.

Lenz, Hermann. *John Dennis, Sein Leben und Seine Werke* (*John Dennis, His Life and His Works*). Marburg: The author, 1913. Painstaking, often plodding investigation of Dennis's life and writings to 1705.

The Life of Mr. John Dennis, the Renowned Critick. London: J. Roberts, 1734. First posthumous account; entertaining collection of anecdotes and evaluation.

Monk, Samuel H. *The Sublime: A Study of Critical Theories in XVIII-Century England.* 1935. Reprint. Ann Arbor: University of Michigan Press, 1960. The most complete and learned discussion of Dennis's contributions to the tradition of a major critical topic.

Morris, David B. *The Religious Sublime: Christian Poetry and Critical Tradition in 18th-Century England.* Lexington: University Press of Kentucky, 1972. Persuasive description of Dennis as the first English theorist of the religious sublime.

Nicolson, Marjorie Hope. *Mountain Gloom and Mountain Glory: The Development of the Aesthetics of the Infinite.* 1959. Reprint. New

York: W. W. Norton, 1963. Insightful analysis of how Dennis formulated his distinction between the sublime and the beautiful after he saw the Alps.

Paul, H. G. *John Dennis: His Life and Criticism.* 1911. Reprint. New York: AMS Press, 1966. The only biographical-critical study touching on all periods of Dennis's life and (despite the title) nearly all of his writings. Although outdated in critical method and information, to date the best overall introduction.

Shawcross, John T. "John Dennis." In *A Milton Encyclopedia.* Edited by William B. Hunter et al. 8 vols. Lewisburg, Pa.: Bucknell University Press, 1978–80, 2:141–43. The best introduction to Dennis's thoughts on and creative uses of Milton.

Whincop, Thomas. *Scanderbeg. . . . To Which Are Added a List of All the Dramatic Authors.* London: W. Reeve, 1747. The second posthumous biographical-critical account; sympathetic; more trustworthy than the 1734 *Life.*

2. Articles

Albrecht, W. P. "John Dennis and the Sublime Pleasures of Tragedy." *Studies on Voltaire and the Eighteenth Century* 87 (1972):65–85. Insightful; Dennis's focus on "enthusiastick" passions, their link with tragedy, and the place of emotion in seeing truth anticipates Hazlitt's and Keats's identification of sublimity and tragedy.

Heffernan, James A. W. "Wordsworth and Dennis: The Discrimination of Feelings." *PMLA* 82 (1967):430–36. Intriguing exploration of how *The Grounds of Criticism* helped Wordsworth define poetic feeling.

Hooker, Edward N. "Pope and Dennis." *ELH* 7 (1940):188–98. Important argument that Dennis wrote *A True Character of Mr. Pope* but otherwise after 1711 published nothing against Pope until provoked to issue *Remarks upon Pope's Homer.*

————. "An Unpublished Autograph Manuscript of John Dennis." *ELH* 1 (1934):156–62. Bibliographical analysis of *The Causes of the Decay and Defects,* dating the essay and assessing the critic's method of writing.

Kramer, Dale. "Passion in Poetic Theory: John Dennis and Wordsworth." *Neuphilologische Mitteilungen* 69 (1968):421–27. Cryptic yet thoughtful review of Dennis's scattered remarks on passion, which Wordsworth adapted in defining poetry.

Logan, Terence P. "Biography in Brief: John Dennis—Critic and Adaptor." *Shakespeare Newsletter* 21, no. 1 (1971):3. Helpful summary of Dennis's career, particularly in drama.

————. "John Dennis's *Select Works,* 1718, 1721." *Papers of the Bibliographical Society of America* 65 (1971):155–56. Bibliographical details about the two issues indicate a decline in Dennis's popularity.

Roberts, William. "John Dennis." *Dictionary of National Biography.* Edited by Leslie Stephen and Sidney Lee. 66 vols. London: Smith, Elder, 1885–1901, 14:369–72. Scholarly reconsideration of the works and biographical facts; the beginning of objective modern research on Dennis.

Rogers, Pat. "New Light on John Dennis." *Notes and Queries* 19 (1972):217–18. Contemporary documents reveal Dennis's financial woes between 1711 and 1715.

Simon, Irene. "John Dennis and Neoclassical Criticism." *Revue Belge de Philosophie et d'Histoire* 56 (1978):663–77. Valuable argument that Dennis's critical writings reveal an imbalance, not a tension, between his championship of order and the weight that he places on passion.

Singh, Amrik. "The Argument on Poetic Justice (Addison *versus* Dennis)." *Indian Journal of English Studies* 3 (1962):61–77. Useful review of Dennis's zealous defense of poetic justice against Addison and others.

Thorpe, Clarence DeWitt. "Two Augustans Cross the Alps: Dennis and Addison on Mountain Scenery." *Studies in Philology* 32 (1935):463–82. Close analysis of Dennis's strong emotional response to great mountain scenery.

Tupper, Fred S. "Notes on the Life of John Dennis." *ELH* 5 (1938):211–17. Summarizes valuable information in the Public Record Office about Dennis's family and his activities before 1711.

Tyre, Richard H. "Versions of Poetic Justice in the Early Eighteenth Century." *Studies in Philology* 54 (1957):29–44. Valuable analysis of the subtle differences between Dennis's concept of poetic justice and those of his contemporaries.

Wilkins, A. N. "John Dennis' Stolen Thunder." *Notes and Queries* 201 (1956):425–28. Pope probably invented the anecdote of his opponent's accusing the Drury Lane managers of stealing a machine for making thunder.

————. "Pope and 'Appius.' " *Notes and Queries* 7 (1960):292–94. In *An Essay on Criticism,* Pope attacks Dennis as "Appius" because he finds in the main character of *Appius and Virginia* qualities that he satirizes in Dennis.

————. "Tragedy and 'The True Politicks.' " *Notes and Queries* 204 (1959):390–94. *Liberty Asserted* illustrates Dennis's belief that tragedy should provide political instruction.

3. Dissertations

Ingram, William Henry. "Greek Drama and the Augustan Stage: Dennis, Theobald, Thomson." Ph.D. diss., University of Pennsylvania, 1966. A close analysis particularly of the structural changes that Dennis made in his Euripidean material as he wrote *Iphigenia.*

Richeson, Edward, Jr. "John Dennis as a Psychological Critic." Ph.D. diss., Boston University, 1962. Detailed review of the contemporary psychology of the passions and the concept of passion in the critic's thought.

Wilkins, Arthur Norman. "An Essay on John Dennis's Theory and Practice of the Art of Tragedy Together with the Text of His Tragedy of *Appius and Virginia.*" Ph.D. diss., Washington University, 1953. Painstaking examination of the operation of the author's tragic theories and his use of sources in the play; full explanatory notes.

Index

Addison, Joseph, *32–40,* 78, 96, 130, 110
AEsop, 91–92
Aglionby, William, 2
Alps, 2, *12–13*
Ambrose, Saint, 104
ancients and moderns, 7
Anne, Queen, 78, 96, 100, *102–103,* 123
Arbuthnot, John, 55
Aristotle, 10–12, 27, 29–30, 35, 43, 70–71
Arnold, Matthew, 130
Assassination Plot, 66
Ault, Norman, 51

Barry, Elizabeth, 69–70, 77
Bart, Jean, 122
Battle of the Authors, The, 43
Bedford, Arthur, 22, 24, 79
Betterton, Thomas, 69–70
Bible, The, 103
Blackmore, Richard, 2, 7, 16, *29–32,* 40, 127
Blatant Beast, The, 54
Boileau-Despréaux, Nicolas, 61, 64, 90
Booth, Barton, 40, 44, 55, 57
Boyer, Abel, 5, 75
Bracegirdle, Anne, 77
Branam, George C., 87
Bredvold, Louis I., 130
Burke, Edmund, 130
Burnet, Thomas, 106, *127–28*
Butler, Samuel, 56, 92, 108

Caesar, Julius, 18, *114–16*
Calves' Head Club, 107

Cambridge University, 1, 14–15
Carew, Thomas, 94
Catholicism, 51, 56
Censor Censured, The, 46
Chaucer, Geoffrey, 57
Churchill, John, Duke of Marlborough, 3, 32, 40, 76, *96–97*
Cibber, Colley, 40–41, 44
Cibber, Theophilus, 4, 74, 105, 113
Clayton, Thomas, 109
Collection of Divine Hymns and Poems, A, 105
Collier, Jeremy, 16, *19–24,* 86
comedy, *43–45,* 47, 67–68, 84
Commendatory Verses on the Author of the Two Arthurs, 31–32, 40
Congreve, William, 21–22, 56
Cooper, Anthony Ashley, Earl of Shaftesbury, 45, 130
Coppinger, Matthew, 5
critics, attacks on, 33, 44–45
Cromwell, Henry, 48
Curll, Edmund, 6, 128

Dacier, André, 26–27
Dacier, Anne, 55
Defoe, Daniel, 2, 107
Denham, John, 57
Dennis, Elizabeth, 1
Dennis, Francis, 1
Dennis, John: aid to sailors, 4, *118–22;* benefit performance, 6, 64; birth, 1; continental tour, 2; death, 6; education, 1; finances, 1–4; health, 4; height of career, 3; reputation as wit,

2, 90–91; royal post, 3–4; work as notary public, 3

WORKS—DRAMA:
Appius and Virginia, 48–49, 52, *80–83,* 130
Comical Gallant, The, 83–86
Gibraltar, 78–80
Invader of His Country, The, 40–41, 86–89
Iphigenia, 5, 70–76
Liberty Asserted, 3, 75–78, 101, 124
"Masque of Orpheus and Euridice, The," 80
Plot, and No Plot, A, 31, 66–68
Rinaldo and Armida, 68–70, 80, 111

WORKS—POETRY:
Battle of Ramillia, The, 40, 97
Britannia Triumphans, 3, 80, 96–97
Court of Death, The, 97–99
Monument, The, 94, *99–102*
"Part of the *Te Deum* Paraphras'd," 9, *104–106*
Passion of Byblis, The, 16
"Pindarick Ode on the King, A," 60, 95
Poem upon the Death of . . . Queen Anne, A, 102–103
Poems in Burlesque, 2, 90–91
Reverse, The, 77, *106–108,* 130–31
"To a Painter," 93
"Upon Our Victory at Sea," 94–95

WORKS—PROSE:
Advancement and Reformation of Modern Poetry, The, 3, 7–9, 16, 19, 30, 105, 108, 117

Causes of the Decay and Defects of Dramatick Poetry, The, 11
Characters and Conduct of Sir John Edgar . . . Two Letters, The, 5, *41–43*
Characters and Conduct of Sir John Edgar . . . Third and Fourth Letter, The, 41–43
Critical Works, The, 129–30
Danger of Priestcraft, The, 3, 5, *125–26*
Defence of Sir Fopling Flutter, A, 43–44
Essay on the Genius and Writings of Shakespear, An, 18–19, 34–36, 86–87, 115
Essay on the Navy, An, 118–22, 124
Essay on the Opera's, An, 3, *109–15*
Essay upon Publick Spirit, An, 113–15, 126
Faith and Duties of Christians, The, 127–28
Grounds of Criticism, The, 7–10, 16, 103, 105, 108
Impartial Critick, The, 3, 17, *25–29, 58–59*
Julius Caesar Acquitted, 114–16
Letters upon Several Occasions, 2
Miscellaneous Tracts, 22
"Of Prosody," 108
Original Letters, 22, 32, 39
Person of Quality's Answer to Mr. Collier's Letter, The, 23–24
Priestcraft Distinguish'd from Christianity, 126–27
Proposal for Putting a Speedy End to the War, A, 3, *122–24*
Reflections Critical and Satyrical, 49–52
Remarks on . . . Prince Arthur, 3, 16, *29–32,* 66

Remarks on . . . The Conscious Lovers, 44–46
Remarks on Mr. Pope's Rape of the Lock, 60–62
Remarks upon Cato, 5, 36–39, 52–53
Remarks upon Mr. Pope's Translation of Homer, 55–59
Remarks upon . . . the Dunciad, 16, 63–64
Seamens Case, The, 118, 121–22
Stage Defended, The, 24–25
Treatise Concerning the State of Departed Souls, A, 128
True Character of Mr. Pope, A, 53–55
Usefulness of the Stage, The, 2–3, *19–23,* 33, 110
Vice and Luxury Publick Mischiefs, 116–18

WORKS—VARIED SELECTIONS:
Miscellanies in Verse and Prose, 2, *91–93*
Select Works, The, 5–6, 31, 33, 39, 59, 93, 95, 131

Dennis, Sarah, 1–2
Descartes, René, 12
Dillon, Wentworth, Earl of Roscommon, 50, 105
Dionysius of Halicarnassus, 80
Disraeli, Isaac, 129
Dodington, George, 25
Downes, John, 74–75, 110
Dryden, John, 3, 19, 56, 91, 105, 108

Earbery, Matthias, 128
Eccles, John, 68
Ehrman, John, 122
Elizabeth I, Queen, 83
epic poetry, 29–31

Etherege, George, 43
Euripides, 18, 29, 35, *71–75*
Eve, Simon, 1

Fairfax, Edward, 68
Fielding, Henry, 77
Freeholder's Journal, 45

Gay, John, 14, 55, 83, 91, 110
Gentleman's Journal, 2, 28, 90, 92–94
George I, King, 102
Gildon, Charles, 11, 26, 47, 53, 60, 64, 110–11, 130
Godolphin, Sidney, Earl of Godolphin, 40
Godwin, William, 11
Goldsmith, Oliver, 130
Gordon, Thomas, 114, 116
Greenwood, James, 43, 108

Haines, Joseph, 68
Hanoverian Succession, 40, *103*
Harvey, William, 12
Hazlitt, William, 130
Herrick, Marvin T., 28
Hill, Aaron, 6, 30, 70
Hobbes, Thomas, 12
Homer, 7, 55, *57–59,* 64
Hooker, Edward Niles, 8, 24, 61, 91, *129*
Horace, 10–11, 18, 45, 56, 90
Horne, William, 1
Hughes, John, 101
Hume, Robert, 80

Jacob, Giles, 6, 64, 78, 80, 130
Jacobitism, 50, 56, 66, 68, 86, 130
James II, King, 114
Johnson, Samuel, 9, 11, 14, 17, 129–30
Jonson, Ben, 25, 41, 43, 56, 80
Juvenal, 45, 56, 90

Keats, John, 130
Kippis, Andrew, 74, 105, 112
Kitto, H. D. F., 73

La Fontaine, Jean de, 91–92
Langbaine, Gerard, 8
Law, William, 19, 24–25, 130
Le Bossu, René, 29
L'Estrange, Roger, 91
Life of Mr. John Dennis, The, 6, 68
Lintot, Bernard, 51, 53
Livy, 80
Locke, John, 12, 91
Loftis, John, 130
Longinus, 9, *13,* 59
Louis XIV, King, 75–76, 97, 100, 130

Mandeville, Bernard, 92, *116–18*
Mary II, Queen, 98–99
Middlesex Grand Jury, 2, 22
Milton, John, 7, 9, *16–17,* 19, 32–33, 130
Molière, 43
Montagu, Charles, Earl of Halifax, 32, 40
morality, 3
Motteux, Peter, 90
Mourning Poets, The, 98–99
Muses Mercury, 80

Natives, The, 107
Neoclassicism, 10, *30–31,* 44
Neoplatonism, 10, *14–15,* 109
Newton, Isaac, 12
Nichols, John, 1

Oldfield, Anne, 41
Oldmixon, John, 70
order, 10, 12, 15

passion, 7, 9, *12,* 20–21, 27, 30, 69
Philips, Ambrose, 47–48, 56

Plain Dealer, 105
Plato, 12
Plautus, 18
poetic justice, 11, 25, *33–37*
Pope, Alexander, 5–6, 10, 16, 33, 39, *46–65,* 80, 83, 97, 110, 129–30
Prior, Matthew, 91
Project for the Advancement of the Stage, A, 60
psychology, 12
public service, 3, 40, 71, 75, *128,* 131
puns, 61

religion, 8–9, *14,* 24, 32, 103–104, *124–28*
Richmond, Herbert, 122
Robe, Thomas, 120
Roberts, William, 6, 129
rules, artistic, *10–12,* 38, 41
Rymer, Thomas, 11, *25–28*

Sacheverell, Henry, 5, 42, 56, 102, *124–26,* 130
Sanderson, Thomas, 1
Savile, George, Marquis of Halifax, 119
Scriblerus Club, 14
Shakespeare, William, 12, *16–19,* 25–26, 28, 34, 80, *83–89,* 109
Sheffield, John, Earl of Mulgrave and Duke of Buckingham, 50
Shelley, Percy Bysshe, 130
Shepherd, Fleetwood, 90
Sir Richard Steele . . . Vindicated, 44
Society for Promoting Christian Knowledge, 22
Sophocles, 18, 35
South Sea Bubble, 45
Southey, Robert, 95, 129
Spencer, Hazelton, 85
Spingarn, J. E., 28, 129

Stanhope, James, Earl of Chester-field, 4
Steele, Richard, 4–6, 16, *39–47,* 64, 106
sublime, *12–14,* 16–17
Sutherland, James, 62
Swedenberg, H. T., Jr., 130
Swift, Jonathan, 4, 11, 91, 110

Tasso, Torquato, 9, 68
Tate, Nahum, 86, 90–91
Terence, 18
Theobald, Lewis, 55–56, 64
Tories, 36, 102, 114
tragedy, *20–21,* 25–27, 33–39
Tryal of Skill, The, 3
Tupper, Fred S., 1
Tutchin, John, 106–108

Vanbrugh, John, 6, 19, 21–22, 64
Victor, Benjamin, 47

Villiers, George, Duke of Buck-ingham, 33, 93
Virgil, 7, *29–31*

Waller, Edmund, 26–28
Walpole, Robert, Earl of Orford, 45
Ward, Ned, 107
West, Walter, 40
Whigs, 3, 36, 40, 77–78, 103, 114, 124
Wilks, Robert, 40, 44
William III, King, 19, 40, 86, *99–101,* 106, 114, 127
Will's (coffee house), 2
Wilmot, John, Earl of Rochester, 54
Winstanley, William, 8
Wycherley, William, 48, 51, 67

Young, Edward, 102